SECOND EDITION

A VERY SHORT, FAIRLY INTERESTING AND REASONABLY CHEAP BOOK ABOUT

INTERNATIONAL BUSINESS

GEORGE CAIRNS AND MARTYNA ŚLIWA

Los Angeles | London | New Delhi
Singapore | Washington DC | Melbourne

Los Angeles | London | New Delhi
Singapore | Washington DC | Melbourne

SAGE Publications Ltd
1 Oliver's Yard
55 City Road
London EC1Y 1SP

SAGE Publications Inc.
2455 Teller Road
Thousand Oaks, California 91320

SAGE Publications India Pvt Ltd
B 1/I 1 Mohan Cooperative Industrial Area
Mathura Road
New Delhi 110 044

SAGE Publications Asia-Pacific Pte Ltd
3 Church Street
#10-04 Samsung Hub
Singapore 049483

© George Cairns and Martyna Śliwa 2017

First published in 2008. Reprinted 2009 (twice),
2010, 2011, 2013 and 2016
This second edition published 2017

Editor: Matthew Waters
Assistant editor: Lyndsay Aitken
Production editor: Sarah Cooke
Marketing manager: Alison Borg
Cover design: Wendy Scott
Typeset by: C&M Digitals (P) Ltd, Chennai, India
Printed by CPI Group (UK) Ltd, Croydon, CR0 4YY

Library of Congress Control Number: 2016955369

British Library Cataloguing in Publication data

A catalogue record for this book is available from
the British Library

ISBN 978-1-47398-100-3
ISBN 978-1-47398-101-0 (pbk)

Contents

About the Authors

George Cairns is Adjunct Professor at QUT Business School, Brisbane. George co-founded and was co-editor of the journal *Critical Perspectives on International Business*. Throughout his writing, George has adopted a critical stance on the impacts of IB activity on remote and excluded stakeholders, both in the present and the future. Much of his work applies scenario methods to explore possible and plausible futures. His studies include a number of journal articles on the shipbreaking industry of Bangladesh. George has published in journals including *Human Relations*, *European Journal of Operational Research*, *Technological Forecasting & Social Change* and *Futures*.

Martyna Śliwa is Professor of Management and Organization Studies at the University of Essex. Her research interests focus on a range of topics relevant to the employees, managers and other stakeholders of contemporary organizations, especially those operating in the international business environment. Examples of Martyna's recent research projects include: language(s) and power in multinational corporations, transnational professional mobility, and the effects of the intersections of nationality and gender on organizational hierarchies and individual careers of highly skilled professionals. Martyna is currently an Associate Editor of *Management Learning*. She has published in journals including *British Journal of Management*, *Journal of International Business Studies*, *Management Learning* and *Organization*.

Acknowledgements

We would like to thank all academic colleagues, students, friends and family who have inspired, guided and encouraged us both in writing this second edition and in our earlier works that inform it. Their contributions have been invaluable. Any errors and omissions in the book are, of course, our own responsibility.

the idea that the trajectory along which IB has developed has not necessarily been a 'natural', 'inevitable' or the only possible route. We highlight the major impact that powerful stakeholders in IB – such as nation states, multinational corporations (MNCs) and supranational institutions – have had, over time, on developing particular types of IB practice and on the spread of theories that legitimize them.

Third, our thinking about the implications of IB for all stakeholders leads us to raise topics and issues of concern to us, and to consider aspects of IB other than the strategies for success of the ubiquitous Apple, Toyota, Walmart and the like. You will find that we discuss aspects of IB such as the working conditions of those who labour in the fields and in sweatshops across the world to produce the foodstuffs, clothing, consumer electronics and other products that pervade supermarkets and shopping malls. In addition, we raise issues such as trade in arms, tax evasion and the impact of consumers on labour governance in global supply chains.

Finally, we introduce a range of frameworks and approaches that you might employ to undertake your own analysis of issues in contemporary IB. Using these, we encourage you to think about possible scenarios for future developments, and what your role might be in bringing about positive change.

Who, then, do we see as the readership of this book? First, we have written it for students of management-related subjects who are looking for a short text that provides an overview of relevant theories and practices of IB. Second, we intend it to be of interest to IB managers who want to understand the conceptual underpinnings of what they do and why certain strategies are proposed for internationalization of the firm. For both of these groups, as we have outlined above, we hope to move thinking beyond simple 'how to' questions. We aim to prompt reflection on issues of 'how things are connected', 'why' and 'with what effect'. We also like to think that our colleagues in the academic community will find this book useful. Finally, we hope that it will be of interest to a wider audience, recognizing that we all, whether as employees, consumers or citizens, impact and are impacted by contemporary IB activities, and have the potential to influence their future
- development.

We realize that, although intended as a 'reasonably cheap' text, this book will not be affordable to potential readers in many countries where the general level of income makes it very expensive. Bearing in mind that its distribution will be set within the confines of the publisher's marketing strategy and that it is written in English by western academics, it will remain inaccessible for the majority of the world population. In writing this short book about international business, we acknowledge that this in itself constitutes an IB project, using resources to generate profit from sales in those markets where demand can be identified.

We trust that, in discussing how everyone contributes to the development of and the problems stemming from IB, we can make you aware of these and stimulate your thinking on how you might, through your own actions, make a difference now for the benefit of future generations.

How to read this book

Since this is a 'very short' book, we cannot cover every aspect of IB in detail. However, we are conscious of the dangers of stereotyping and generalizing inherent in any attempt to provide both a short and a comprehensive account of a discipline. We have been selective in including and excluding material, and we recognize that other authors would have approached the subject from a different standpoint. For example, where we write about the history of IB theory and practice, we present a sequence of conceptual developments and empirical examples. This does not, however, mean that we see history as unfolding in a linear and progressive fashion, or that our chosen examples are exhaustive. We note that there have been certain shifts in thinking over time, about who the main actors in international transactions are, and how changes in technologies have impacted IB practice. However, we do not necessarily consider that these have contributed to an improvement of the situation of many of those affected. To enable you to read beyond our text and to fill in gaps in theory and thinking, we refer you to other sources for more background and more detail. The texts that we point you to represent examples of mainstream IB textbooks, more critical writing on the nature and impact of IB, and other relevant resources that will hopefully enable you to place your own consideration of IB into a broader context.

At this point, we would highlight a number of assumptions that underpin a general understanding of IB. We summarize these as follows:

- It is natural and beneficial for human beings to engage in economic activity.
- The term 'business' corresponds with the actions that people pursue when they undertake this economic activity.
- The rules according to which business takes place are, to a large extent, determined by nation states.

- Contemporarily, the pursuit of IB is linked to the spread of capitalism.
- As a domain of theory and practice, IB is worthy of attention by affected stakeholders, including researchers, educators and students.

To clarify our own approach, we outline a few key terms that we use throughout our text and the broad meaning that we attach to each, acknowledging their grounding in the above assumptions:

International business (IB): We read IB as referring to any form of commercial exchange of materials, goods, services or any other resources that involves transfer across national boundaries. These transactions may be formal and legal, or they may lie outside the confines of formal economy and legality.

Internationalization: In referring to the internationalization of business and of organizations, we point to their expansion beyond their country of origin through establishing relationships, transaction linkages or operations in one or more other countries.

Globalization: The term globalization is subject to many interpretations and has no single agreed meaning. For some, it represents a natural, inevitable and largely unproblematic move towards a 'borderless world' and the end of the independent nation state. Here, we align with those who read it as the spread of western social, economic and cultural values. Intertwined with this process, we see the imperative of MNCs to configure and develop their value chains at a global level in the aim of making the most of their own efficiency and effectiveness in order to maximize their shareholder value.

Neoliberalism: The process of globalization that we describe above is underpinned by the advancement of neoliberal policies. These support the transfer of control over country economies from the public to the private sector, with privatization of state-owned enterprises (SOEs), development of a free market largely devoid of government intervention, and the elimination of restrictions on firms' decision making. The spread of neoliberalism is advocated, and in cases enforced, by Washington-based institutions that include the World Bank and the International Monetary Fund (IMF).

Drawing inspiration from Aristotle

As we have outlined above, our approach to IB is based upon inclusive thinking about all stakeholders. The 'stakeholder approach' was first articulated by Ed Freeman (1984) and it has since been applied in discussions of business ethics and how organizations are responsible not only to their financial investors but also to other parties, and to society at large. However, contemplating the broad consequences of actions for the whole of humanity has a long history. It can be traced back to the Greek philosophers and, in particular, to Aristotle's (350BC/2004) virtue ethics, especially his writings in *The Nicomachean Ethics*. In this work, Aristotle outlines the intellectual virtue of *phronēsis*, generally translated into English as 'practical wisdom' or 'prudence'. Aristotle (350BC/2004: 150) considers *phronēsis* as an individual trait necessary 'to be able to deliberate about what is good and advantageous', and to be 'capable of action with regard to things that are good or bad'. *Phronēsis* implies concern for the good of humanity at large, including present and future generations. The concept has been applied by contemporary writers (e.g. Cairns and Śliwa, 2008; Dunne, 1993; Shotter and Tsoukas, 2014) to address problems of ethics, governance and the impact of the actions of groups and individuals on others. For example, Bent Flyvbjerg (2001: 60) offers a way of approaching inquiry into social phenomena in accordance with *phronēsis* by first asking four seemingly simple questions:

Where are we going?

Is this development desirable?

What, if anything, should we do about it?

Who gains and who loses, and by which mechanisms of power?

In writing this book, we bear in mind these four questions in relation to various aspects of the theory and practice of IB. We draw upon *phronēsis* to generate discussion from the perspective of a broad range of stakeholders, and to support an understanding of IB theories and activities in terms of their origins, emergence, outcomes and implications. More specifically, in Chapter 7 we show the application of phronetic inquiry to critically appraise current developments, and to explore potential future IB scenarios and their possible impacts for all stakeholders.

Stakeholders in international business

In the following three chapters of this book, we explain how the theories of international business that have developed over time have placed the benefit of, first, the nation state and then, more recently, the firm as the key concern of IB. We draw your attention not only to countries and companies, but also to those who are often seen as either marginal to IB practice, or as factors to be 'managed' for the benefit of commercial organizations. Moving beyond the country- or firm-centred approaches, we question the frequently taken-for-granted notion that the underpinning purpose of capitalist organizations is to maximize profits and return on investment for financial stakeholders. The proponents of this assumption often quote the renowned econo-mist Milton Friedman (1962: 133), who stated that:

> There is one and only one social responsibility of business – to use its resources and engage in activities designed to increase its profits so long as it stays within the rules of the game, which is to say, engages in open and free competition, without deception or fraud ... for corporate officials to make as much money for their stockholders as possible.

What is often missed out of the discussion, however, are topics that Friedman himself raised as a counterpoint to the profit motive of pri-vate enterprise, namely the duty of the state to attend to matters of health, education and defence, and the question of who looks after the interests of the worker, the consumer and broader society. Below, we briefly discuss some of the impacts of IB on these three categories of stakeholders. Further, we reflect upon what we identify as problematic issues that ought to be addressed in the context of Flyvbjerg's frame-work of four questions for developing an analysis in accordance with *phronēsis*.

The worker and international business

In thinking about the relationship between the worker and the interna-tional business organization, we believe it is important to look at the effects of MNCs on all types and levels of employees – both their own and those of their supplier and client organizations – at a global level. In so doing, we draw attention to issues of socio-economic inequality and poverty, and of exploitation associated with internationalization and globalization of business.

Nowadays, it is common practice for MNCs to configure their 'value chain' internationally or globally, seeking to gain 'competitive advantage' (Porter, 1985) over their competitors through minimizing production costs. In so-called 'developed economies', labour has long been recognized as the major contributor to overall costs of production. This has led firms to shift their production activities to locations that offer cheaper labour, both in terms of wages paid and of infrastructure provision and employee benefits. The existence of such locations, which are the result of structural discrepancies across countries and regions, underpins the possibilities for attaining competitive advantage through exploitation of global cost differentials. Companies that have moved some or all aspects of their product or service delivery to countries with low costs of employment have a vested interest in maintaining these differentials, whilst 'developing economies' that aspire to gain a foothold on the ladder of economic growth are prepared to market themselves as providers of cheap labour, low- or no-cost factories, and tax-free investment opportunities. Both the MNCs that seek out such locations and those countries that offer such opportunities continue to do so despite the problematic impact that this 'race to the bottom' may have on local populations.

Critical commentators draw attention to the growing inequalities between and within societies as a result of globalization and the development of new models of supply that take advantage of economic differences – for example, using sweatshop labour in one country to produce branded goods that generate high levels of profit when sold in another. This fragmentation of global production results in social exclusion and impoverishment for many, with a simultaneous formation of global 'elites'; the social and economic 'winners' of globalization. At the end of the previous century, Zygmunt Bauman (1998: 72) stated that, in this age of globalized production and consumption, 'the new rich do not need the poor any more'. But, as you will find as you read on, we consider that the dynamics of contemporary IB – in domains such as production, consumption, investment and disposal – is very much about complex interdependencies between the rich and the poor, even when these groups do not directly interact. Where the wealthy factory owner of the past lived in geographic proximity to his workers, the super-rich of today are globally mobile and can live in London or Dubai while they generate income in Dhaka or Shenzhen. In any of these settings, they can remain detached from the workers on whom they rely for wealth generation. The gap between the wealth and mobility of the world's rich and that of the poor takes us to a consideration of another group affected by IB activity, consumers.

The consumer and international business

While shareholders are the focus of profit distribution for MNCs, consumers are the main group through which these profits are generated.

As a consequence, individuals external to commercial organizations are mainly conceptualized as actual and potential consumers, rather than as members of society. Critics of the consumer discourse contend that by referring to people as 'consumers' companies disregard other social roles of individuals. At the same time, its proponents argue that through concentrating on the needs of the consumer, firms not only meet these needs, but also provide the major engine of economic growth and development that will ultimately benefit everyone globally. The core of this argument is that we all aspire to increase our material wealth and that, as we progress through various stages of economic development, all members of all societies will ultimately achieve this goal. Some commentators point out how, just as members of society in developed economies have benefited from the growth of international trade in the nineteenth and twentieth centuries to become the consumer, so too those of Brazil, China, India and other emerging economies will become the new consumers of the twenty-first century. With other critics, we question the veracity and morality of this view of consumption.

We see two very different problems with conceptualizing people exclusively as consumers of the company's products and services. First, this approach means that those who do have high levels of disposable income are targeted with ever more innovative products and services, regardless of whether these actually contribute to the improvement of people's quality of life, and of the environmental impacts of this increased consumption. Here, those with low income levels are ignored, even though they might have important needs for products and services. Second, where individuals with low disposable income are the targeted market for products and services, they are vulnerable to exploitation. We discuss this in more detail in Chapter 6.

Society and international business

As we have pointed out above, the effects of international business on society at large give rise to issues of social and economic inequality and exploitation. We look first at some of the historical examples of such exploitation and how their legacy continues to this day. Early examples of IB include the transportation of entire populations from Africa to the Americas to be sold into slavery, to work on the cotton and tobacco plantations, or in service for the rich European settlers. Although the transportation of slaves was officially ended some 200 years ago, the descendants of those who were forcibly taken from their homeland across the Atlantic Ocean later provided a major part of the workforce of emerging US manufacturing industries. Whereas the slave trade was conducted around the Atlantic rim, Europeans in Asia developed another form of international trade based upon exploitation and misery, in this case through trading opium.

In the present day, we identify similar issues of the exploitation of groups in broad society where, as outlined above, people are seen as potential or actual consumers of a company's products and services, or as parts of the global workforce for their provision. We discuss the social and economic changes that have accompanied the development of IB, and how they affect society today. In addition to issues of socio-economic exclusion and increasing poverty, we discuss societal impacts of new products and services that have become available with the advancement of technology, specifically the global spread of the Internet.

Organization of this book

We have divided this book into seven chapters. In Chapter 1, we discuss the historical origins of IB, giving an overview of both classical and neo-classical theories of international trade and providing illustrations of the types of activity that exemplified early forms of IB exchange. We present both those explanatory theories that are considered to be part of the canon of IB and those that offer a critical counterpoint, and are often excluded from discussions of the conceptual underpinnings of the discipline in mainstream textbooks. Chapter 2 continues with consideration of theoretical developments into the twentieth century. We point to a shift of focus in thinking about IB from viewing the nation state as the key actor to the rise of MNCs as central to IB activity. We discuss forms of investment in support of MNC growth and the search for competitive advantage, profit maximization and shareholder return. Through reference to more critical theoretical appraisals, we also problematize the implications of the centrality of the firm in IB knowledge and practice. In Chapter 3 we introduce the key institutions of contemporary IB, considering the role and status of the International Monetary Fund (IMF), the World Bank and the World Trade Organization (WTO). We do this to facilitate understanding of the political and economic conditions underlying the growth of various structures of economic cooperation and integration. In engaging with different perspectives on the impact of these institutions, we open up a discussion of their role in light of ongoing conditions of trade imbalance and global economic inequalities. The origin and development of MNCs is the subject of

Chapter 4. Here, we highlight the powerful position of MNCs not only in the field of business, but also in the areas of politics, society and environment. We illustrate the problematic nature of corporate financial success in relation to broader socio-economic impacts. This is followed by a discussion of the more recent developments in IB environment in Chapter 5. Specifically, we elaborate on the impact of accelerating technological change and socio-political and economic disruption, with examples ranging from the global financial crisis (GFC) to the emergence of new Internet-based business models. The focus of Chapter 6 is on how organizations operating within the IB environment deal with people. We return to and explore in detail the ways in which MNCs and other businesses affect the lives of a range of stakeholders – individuals and groups who might be their direct employees but also customers, workers employed throughout global supply chains, and members of local communities, often remote and excluded. We also draw attention to the interconnectedness of stakeholders in IB. Having provided a grounding in the theories and practices of IB from its historical roots to the present day, in Chapter 7 we outline some analytic frameworks for developing an understanding of how contemporary organizations relate to their broad environment, socially, economically and ecologically. Through application of these, you will be able to explore the range of possible and plausible futures for any IB activity, along with the potential impacts of these for all involved and affected stakeholders.

Throughout this book, we hope to challenge you to consider the implications and impact of IB as it is currently constituted, with its drive for continual business growth and expansion. We seek to inspire your own critical reflection on the nature of IB as well as the actual and potential influence we all have on its future direction and purpose. It is not our intention to moralize, but we feel it is necessary to present ideas, practices, theories and critiques of IB from a range of perspectives beyond what we see as a 'business-as-usual' approach, in order to stimulate reflection on why IB is as it is, and on how it might be different.

1

Classical and Neo-classical Theories of International Trade

In this chapter, we discuss the historical origins of IB in terms of both theory and practice. We feel that in order to fully understand contemporary IB, it is necessary to have knowledge of the chronological development and theoretical underpinnings of the discipline, and of the ways in which IB practices have evolved to become key constituents of present-day capitalism and globalization. Through questioning often unstated assumptions behind theories of IB and through discussion of alternative perspectives on history and theory, we seek to stimulate your thinking on a broader range of issues relating to the social, political and environmental impacts of IB practices. We hope to inspire you to question the neoliberal globalization agenda that underpins dominant understandings of IB. The two main types of activity within IB are classified as 'international trade' and 'international investment'. Historically, international trade, involving commercial exchange of goods or services across boundaries, developed prior to international investment, that is the movement of capital between nations. Early theories of international trade that we address in this chapter include mercantilism, physiocratism, the theory of absolute advantage, the theory of comparative advantage, and the pure theory of trade. In addition, we discuss the early twentieth-century development of the theory of factor endowments. After presenting an overview of these theories and their practical implications, we discuss the challenges to them that arose from alternative thinking on socio-political issues at the end of the nineteenth century and in the early part of the twentieth century. These are, by and large, rooted in the writings of Karl Marx on the political economy.

███████ The origins of international trade theory

International trade has existed for millennia, and examples of what we now call 'IB transactions' can be traced back to the days of the

Phoenician Empire. The earliest forms of IB were based on exchange of tangible goods, such as agricultural produce or luxury items like spices, silk and amber. The latter two gave their names to great trade routes that traversed continents: the Silk Road and the Amber Road. The first of these connected China with India, Mesopotamia, Persia, Egypt and Rome. The second provided a conduit for transporting amber from the North Sea and Baltic coasts across Europe to Italy, Greece, the Black Sea region and Egypt. As these trade routes developed in Europe and Asia, the indigenous peoples of Australasia and the Americas also travelled across land and sea to engage in the exchange of goods.

While the origins of international trade were not confined to one geographical location, the theoretical underpinnings of contemporary IB stem from thinking that originated in Europe. From Columbus' arrival in the Americas in 1492, and even earlier, foundations were laid for the development of capitalism as a political and economic system that requires geographical expansion in order to create wider possibilities for capital accumulation, through enabling exploitation of resources and market opportunities beyond the home economy. Historically, with the rise of capitalism came theories explaining and legitimizing the need for countries to grow politically and economically beyond their original boundaries. 'Mercantilism', which emerged as the dominant school of economic thought in Europe from the sixteenth to the eighteenth century, coincided with the move away from a feudal society, the emergence of the nation state, and colonial expansion of European powers during a period of global exploration and the 'discovery' of new lands. The rate of development accelerated from the seventeenth century with population growth, particularly in urban areas, and advancements – first in shipping and then railway technology – that provided the capability for the expansion of production and trade.

Principles of mercantilism

The basic principle of mercantilism was that a state – understood as the government and the treasury – should aim to maximize its wealth through sale of goods to other countries. This followed the economic logic of the 'zero sum game' and implied that the country that exported finished products should be the sole beneficiary, at the expense of the importer. The objective of trade was to support the accumulation of precious metals – the key measure of national wealth – obtained in exchange for exported goods.

Mercantilism represented the interests of governments and merchants engaged in trade and, at the same time, it disadvantaged the labouring and farming classes. The ongoing social and economic poverty of these groups was seen as desirable, since any increase in their spending power, free time or levels of education was viewed as detrimental to productivity, and hence to the nation's economy.

Within the mercantile system, the nation also enhanced its prosperity by application of selective export subsidies, coupled with import duties, tariffs and other restrictions. In practice, employment of mercantilist trade principles resulted in conflict between nation states, each seeking to gain control over land and resources and to secure the greatest share of what was considered a finite volume of trade in the world. Thus, the philosophy of mercantilism played a role in legitimizing the spread of European imperialism and in sparking the outbreak of European conflicts between the sixteenth and eighteenth centuries. The war between France and the Netherlands of 1672 was held, in part at least, to be due to France's imposition of duties on a wide range of foreign produce, leading to Dutch retaliation in prohibiting the import of French wines, brandies and other goods.

Early critics of mercantilism questioned the assumption of trade being a zero sum game and pointed to the possibility of both partners in an exchange benefiting from it. They also highlighted the weaknesses of some of the other theoretical assumptions of mercantilism, that we do not have the space to discuss here. However, worth noting is the lack of critical response to mercantilism's privileging of some groups in society over others. Rather, the focus remained on ideas about how best to promote the economic good of the nation state. Following these early criticisms of mercantilism, more comprehensive critiques of the mercantile system were offered by the French physiocrats and by the Scot, Adam Smith.

Responses to mercantilism – physiocratism and Adam Smith's theory of absolute advantage

Today, despite the rhetoric of trade liberalization and economic openness, we can identify influences of mercantilism in the application of protectionist policies by countries, including China, Japan and the USA, and by trading blocs such as the European Union. Governments still seek to promote exports, to discourage and reduce imports and, in some cases, will pursue a nationalist agenda and encourage the purchase of domestically produced goods. Historically, as early as the second half of the eighteenth century, the entire notion of the development of wealth through trade was rejected by the French 'physiocrats' who believed that a nation's wealth was generated by domestic agricultural production. The physiocrats emphasized the role of farm workers as the 'productive' class, whom they distinguished from the 'proprietary' class of landowners and the 'sterile' class of artisans and merchants. The origin and popularity of physiocratism in France at this point in history is not surprising, since the country's economy was based upon agricultural rather than industrial production. In the second half of the twentieth century, the emergence and reinforcement of the European Common Agricultural Policy might be seen as the fallout of the French historically favouring agriculture over manufacturing.

In the late eighteenth century, mercantilism was superseded by the free market economics of Adam Smith (1776/1999), first set out in his seminal work *An Inquiry into the Nature and Causes of the Wealth of Nations*. When this work was first published, Britain was the world's most highly developed capitalist economy, and the new 'industrial barons' seized upon Smith's ideas about the necessity of freeing business from government control. They saw his theories as enabling them to import raw materials and to expand their exports of manufactured goods without restriction. At the same time, for the poor in society, Smith's free exchange gave the promise of access to cheap imports – in his time, specifically, grain. Smith's *Wealth of Nations* is regarded as the foundation of classical economics and as one of the most profound rationales for liberal, capitalist economics. As the most influential thinker in the history of capitalist economics, Smith's work had an impact on later economic theories, from those of Malthus and Ricardo, who built upon his thinking, to those of Karl Marx, who drew upon it in developing his critique of capitalism.

Smith posited that government restrictions on economic freedom, such as tariffs and restrictive trade treaties, contributed to the increasing wealth of merchants, but constrained development and hence did not benefit the growing population at large. Smith criticized most forms of governmental intervention in economic matters, arguing that the role of government should be to provide educational, judicial, military and other institutional frameworks that were not profitable for private enterprise. Smith also believed that individuals are driven by selfishness and greed and that, at the level of the whole economy, this will lead to a broader range of products and services being offered and to prices being driven down, with increased availability to the benefit of all. Smith referred to the mechanism through which this happens as the 'invisible hand' of the market, which balances production and the utilization of goods to the advantage of all. In his explanation of how the invisible hand of the market works, Smith made a link between greed and selfishness as motivators of human actions, and benefits for the whole society as the outcome of these actions – in other words, a link between the creation of profit and the generation of common good. The entire canon of classical economics is based upon this idea. However, the fact that over the years, more and more wealth has been generated globally has not meant that everybody's situation has improved. While the World Bank (2015) highlights falling numbers for those living in absolute poverty, millions of people still starve, have no access to clean water, and cannot afford healthcare and education. At the same time, the disparity between rich and poor continues to increase: by 2016, 1% of the world's population had more wealth than the remaining 99% (Oxfam, 2016). This suggests that the capitalist system, rooted in the principles of economic freedom, has yet to deliver the promised common good. Nevertheless, it is important to discuss Smith's ideas regarding international trade exchange because of their historical and present-day impacts.

Smith's (1776/1999: 33) views on foreign trade were an extension of his principle that it is 'the maxim of every prudent master of a family, never to attempt to make at home what it will cost him more to make than buy'. Smith reasoned that countries should specialize in the production of goods for which they could achieve a low unit cost of production and import them if it was cheaper to do so than to produce them domestically. This reasoning underpins his 'theory of absolute advantage'. As Smith (1776/1999: 35) argued:

> By means of glasses, hotbeds and hot walls, very good grapes can be raised in Scotland, and very good wine too can be made of them at about thirty times the expense for which at least equally good wine can be brought from foreign countries. Would it be a reasonable law to prohibit the importation of all foreign wines merely to encourage the making of claret and burgundy in Scotland?

Smith saw the possibility of all states gaining some form of advantage as a result of exporting goods that they could produce more efficiently than any other and, at the same time, importing those for which another country held 'absolute advantage' through its production efficiency. In general, he was against restrictions on trade and government intervention in the economy, except in a few instances where national security was held to be paramount. While Smith assumed that the invisible hand of the market would ultimately lead to benefit for every member of society, the basic principles of his theory of economic liberalism were subject to challenge and critique by Karl Marx and others from the second half of the nineteenth century. We will return to these arguments later in the chapter.

Beyond Smith – theory of comparative advantage

Early critics of Smith's work argued that examples of absolute advantage are rare, since few countries possess a monopolistic hold over the production capability for any given commodity. In addition, some pointed out that Smith had not considered the situation where two countries might both benefit from trade exchange with each other, even where one holds absolute advantage over the other in the production of all goods. This situation is addressed in the 'theory of comparative advantage', first referred to in Robert Torrens' (1815) *Essay on the External Corn Trade* and formalized by David Ricardo (1817) through a numerical example provided in his book *On the Principles of Political Economy and Taxation*. While the theory of comparative advantage has become one of the most important concepts in international trade theory, it has remained one of the most commonly misunderstood. We realize that for those who have not previously had much exposure to economic theory, an attempt to grasp the logic of the theory of comparative advantage may not, at first sight, seem like a very exciting task. However, as this part of international trade theory informs the understanding both of later developments and of much of the critique of these, we will spend some time explaining the logic behind it in simple terms. In doing this, we stress the significance of two concepts: 'opportunity cost' and 'comparative advantage'.

Ricardo's example refers to a hypothetical situation in which there are only two countries (for convenience called England and Portugal), two goods being produced (cloth and wine) and only one factor of production, namely labour. In contrast to Smith, who only considered the possibility that each of the countries was more productive in one of the commodities than the other, Ricardo conceived the situation in which one – Portugal – was more efficient in the production of both. For Smith, such a situation could not be seen as resulting in an advantageous exchange for England. However, Ricardo showed that, despite Portugal's advantage in both goods, it remains possible for both countries to benefit from trade exchange, where each country specializes in the production of one of them. He also considered that the overall supply of both products would increase, compared to the situation before specialization and trade. According to this reasoning, the choice of which commodity each country should specialize in is not determined by a simple comparison of the costs of production between countries, as defined by the cost of labour. Rather, as Ricardo argued, it is necessary to take account of the 'opportunity costs' of producing both goods in both countries. The opportunity cost of producing cloth versus wine is the amount of wine output that will not be generated as a result of freeing up resources for the production of a unit of cloth. If, for example, Portugal is twice as efficient as England in the production of cloth, but three times as efficient in the production of wine, then it has comparative advantage in wine. At the same time, however, if England must relinquish less wine than would Portugal in order to manufacture one additional unit of cloth, it holds comparative advantage over Portugal in the production of cloth. Following this logic, if Portugal specializes and trades in the goods for which it is 'most better' than England in production efficiency, and England focuses on producing that for which it is 'least worse' than Portugal, both countries will benefit from specialization and exchange.

Ricardian theory can explain how things *might* happen in an ideal world. However, there are several problematic assumptions that underpin it. Some of these are of a theoretical nature, such as the assumptions about the existence of only two countries, labour being the only factor of production, and the trade exchange taking place under conditions of perfect competition. Perhaps more crucially, we would take issue with the major ideological assumptions that Ricardian thinking shares with the ideas of Adam Smith, that is that economic activity driven by the desire to generate profits will bring about positive outcomes for everybody in society.

The impact of classical theories of trade on contemporary IB practice

Early theorizations of economic protectionism and liberalism, as exemplified in mercantilism and the ideas of Adam Smith, are linked to specific instruments of government trade policy that have not only played an important role historically, but remain of significance at the present time. These classical theories underpin the current dominant paradigm that sees international business as an inherently 'good' project and, as such, these early theories give insights into fundamental assumptions that underpin contemporary international business theory and practice. They have also informed a range of developments in organization and management over time.

If we consider how mercantile ideas are used to provide legitimization for protectionist policies by nations, we can identify them as underlying the most common justifications of government intervention in international trade. These include: the protection of infant industries and the promotion of industrialization, the protection of jobs – particularly those that are lower paid and require lower skill levels – in the domestic market, consumer protection – especially for reasons of health and safety, and the protection of national interests. The final category encapsulates action in supporting industries considered as being of strategic importance, such as defence suppliers, or those that have the potential of becoming globally competitive, as well as government implementation of foreign policy, and protection of national identity and culture.

If we look more closely at specific instruments that underpin policies of international trade, both historically and contemporarily, we see that nation states have applied both 'tariff' and 'non-tariff' tools. The former are represented by import duties, whereby government places a tax on foreign produce. As a result, its price is raised above that at which the home country supplier provides it. Since the imported goods become more expensive compared to the domestically produced equivalent, consumers are more likely to purchase goods delivered by home-country firms, and hence, domestic producers are protected from foreign competition. At the same time, the government of the country benefits from duties paid on those goods that are imported. For example, in 2016 the USA imposed a 266% duty on Chinese steel imports, intended to punish alleged 'dumping' – i.e. selling below cost – to increase market share (Miller and Mauldin, 2016).

Non-tariff barriers include import quotas, voluntary export restraints (VERs) and subsidies. Import quotas restrict the amount of a specified product that may be brought into the country, again generally to offer a degree of protection to domestic producers. Common examples of quota application include restrictions by Japan and South Korea on the importation of rice, and by China on sugar imports. In contrast to import quotas, VERs are implemented by the exporter through a bilateral agreement with the target market government. The most commonly quoted example of VERs relates to the limits on exportation of automobiles from Japan to various western countries in the 1980s and 1990s, with the aim of protecting home industries in these countries. Subsidies are a form of barrier to trade implemented by governments to promote the competitiveness of domestic industries in export markets, or to protect their domestic market position. The issue of agricultural subsidies has long been the subject of intergovernmental dispute, accusation and counter-accusation. The European Union has claimed that the USA subsidizes its wheat industry excessively and, at the same time, the USA has argued that the European Common Agricultural Policy (CAP) similarly favours European farmers. In both cases, the argument is that domestic producers are protected from external competition by being enabled to continue with production that would otherwise be economically non-viable. As the EU and USA accuse each other of unfair practices, so non-governmental organizations (NGOs) concerned about international development issues say that both protect their home agribusiness, thereby excluding access to markets by developing countries while, simultaneously, enabling overproduction of commodities that are then 'dumped' in developing countries to the detriment of their own farmers.

Classical economics continues to influence policies and practices within IB. In developing his theory of absolute advantage, Smith grounded his thinking in the 'labour theory' of value – that the value of any good is a function of the amount of labour needed for its production – and he put forward the idea of the division of labour as a way of increasing production efficiency. In contrast to craft production, where one individual would produce a complete commodity, the division of labour involves splitting production into discrete elements, each of which is completed by a different semi-skilled worker. Smith expanded this reasoning from consideration of individual specialization to that of whole nations. His ideas have underpinned a vast array of changes in trade and industry, with a rapid acceleration of key trends in the second half of the twentieth century.

After the Second World War, the emergence and growth of 'new' economies, particularly in South East Asia, was linked to the decline of traditional production industries in developed economies. This trend was seen first in the UK, then across Europe, despite the continuing existence – to start with, at least – of expertise and the means of production. A prime example of this can be seen in the area of shipbuilding, where the UK was the world leader through the nineteenth and first half of the twentieth centuries. As the new economies built up their human and material production resources, they began to undercut the production costs of UK shipbuilding, while maintaining the quality necessary to ship owners. Both Japan and South Korea contributed to the virtual demise of a UK industry that had dominated the world, and the riverfronts of major cities such as Belfast, Glasgow and Newcastle.

The theory of comparative advantage, with its main argument that international trade can increase the welfare of all countries, continues to influence the thinking of those individuals and agencies that promote the need for ever-increasing transnational trade and investment.

Despite its unrealistic assumptions, the principles of Ricardian theory have been used to argue that specialization and free trade are beneficial since they lead to improvements in production and consumption efficiency. In addition, they have been deployed to suggest that less developed economies can compete in the global marketplace through seeking to identify and exploit those areas in which they hold comparative advantage over developed economies. Such exhortations, however, ignore the reality of a world in which the power and impact of political and economic agents are inescapable. In the contemporary world of international trade, even 'low cost' economies now lose out to 'even lower' cost areas of production. As China moves to become a service economy with higher wage levels, a greater proportion of global garment production shifts to lower cost South East Asian countries. Similarly, low labour cost countries such as Bangladesh, India and Pakistan compete for their share of the global market for redundant ship dismantling, as major shipowning companies continue to defy the Basel Convention on the Control of Transboundary Movements of Hazardous Wastes and Their Disposal (usually known as the Basel Convention).

Despite the apparent negative impacts, the basic implication of classical theories of international trade is that, thanks to exchange, more wealth will be created and consumption levels will increase, and will be able to do so beyond the limits of possibility for domestic production alone. While questions about how to tackle poverty and inequality within and between nations remain unanswered within these theories, the prospects of general wealth creation and higher consumption levels are unproblematically viewed as positive, and as a motivator for capitalist development and for countries' engagement in international trade. Only in recent years, with the realization of the global impacts of pollution, resource depletion and climate change, has this assumption been challenged.

Neo-classical theories – expanding free trade doctrine

The theories of trade that we have discussed so far were all based on the economics of supply, with the assumption that the value of commodities was dependent upon the cost of labour involved in their production. The French economist Jean Baptiste Say (1803/2001) was the first to move away from the labour theory of value, laying the ground for what later became known as 'equilibrium analysis'. In its advanced form, in 'neo-classical economics' developed by Jevons (1871), Menger (1871/1950) and Walras (1874) during the second half of the nineteenth century, we find the first suggestion that the price of a commodity is determined not only by the costs of production, but also by the 'utility' obtained by the consumer. Consumers are recognized as making choices of whether or not to buy any particular product at a given price and, through such choices, to influence the allocation of resources by producers in search of efficiency maximization. In relation to international exchange, neo-classical economics embraced the 'pure theory of trade', first expounded by Alfred Marshall (Marshall and Marshall, 1879/1994), which promoted a free market and open competition, and which incorporated consideration of both producer and consumer behaviour.

Pure trade theory incorporated the idea of 'consumer preferences' into a discussion of international trade. Analytically, it relied upon the use of mathematics in developing quantitative models of exchange. Geometric diagrams were used to show how gains from international trade could be achieved by the trading parties. Here, it is not our intention to explain the mathematical formulae behind the models of exchange rooted in the pure theory of trade. Despite their greater sophistication, neo-classical trade theories remained grounded in the same assumption as the classical ones, that capitalist development under the conditions of the free market economy – including the liberalization of trade – will serve the general interests of the entire society. On a theoretical level, this problem is addressed by more recent writings stemming from the Marxist tradition, to which we will return later in this chapter.

While the doctrine of free trade between nations was central to classical and neo-classical theories, in practice, its take-up by individual countries was, at best, patchy, and closely allied to the broader context surrounding prevailing economic and political circumstances. Britain was at the centre of the nineteenth-century free trade movement, lowering tariffs by 20% in the years from 1840 to 1880. However, some economic historians have argued that this happened not so much under the influence of the thinking of Smith and others, but because government was able to raise funds through other means, in particular through income tax drawn from the expanding population working in its burgeoning industries.

Other European countries did not adopt universal free trade principles and, in supporting international trade development, relied to a great extent upon reciprocal trade agreements with preferred partners, known as 'most favoured nations' (MFNs). By the late 1860s, such agreements had been adopted by the majority of European nations. Even though MFN status involved the liberalization of trade, it was often conferred for political rather than purely economic reasons. France, for example, entered into a bilateral free trade agreement with Prussia with the intention of acting against the interests of Austria-Hungary. As European nations moved towards freer trade regimes, the United States remained more protectionist and continued to maintain import duties on a wide variety of products up to the 1880s.

While European bilateral trade pacts were negotiated on a partnership basis, both Britain and the United States used 'gunboat diplomacy' to force open markets in Asia. After the first Opium War with China, Britain initially occupied Hong Kong, then negotiated its ceding from China to Britain. After the second Opium War, Britain set up free trade in Chinese ports such as Shanghai. Similarly, the USA sent Commodore Matthew Perry's fleet of 'black ships' to force Japan to abandon its closed economy, to end a 200-year exclusive trading partnership with the Netherlands, and to engage in free trade exchange with the USA under the 1854 Treaty of Peace and Amity.

Theory of factor endowments

The final stage of development of country-based theories of international trade was Heckscher (1919/1950) and Ohlin's (1933/1967) 'theory of factor endowments'. Heckscher and Ohlin argued that comparative advantage of one country over another in the production of a given commodity stems from the relative abundance of the factor that is more intensely utilized in its production. In its original form, the model assumed only two factors of production (labour and capital), two commodities and two countries (2x2x2). Based upon this basic model, if one country has an abundance of labour relative to the other, it will export labour-intensive goods, whereas if it is relatively labour-scarce, it will import these. Likewise, if it is relatively capital-rich, it will concentrate its exports in those products that require high capital input. The initial version of the Heckscher–Ohlin theory, with its simplistic reliance on the 2x2x2 framework, was later developed to incorporate more realistic assumptions, such as the introduction of further factors of production (e.g. land) and consideration of the role of tariffs in shaping patterns of international trade.

The Heckscher–Ohlin theory has been influential in international economics because of the explanation it offers to the question about the source of comparative advantage, moving beyond the classical labour theory of value and enabling a range of factors of production to be considered. However, despite its strong appeal at a theoretical level, the assumptions behind the theory of factor endowments have turned out to be problematic and, at an empirical level, its relevance has been limited. Nevertheless, faced with the option of rejecting factor endowments theory or seeking to explain its failings, many economists have followed the latter route, being unwilling to give up its high theoretical significance within neo-classical economics.

Even though the results of these attempts have been inconclusive, knowledge of assumptions inherent in the Heckscher–Ohlin model has implications for understanding contemporary international business. For example, the model assumes perfect competition in factor and production markets, and lacks consideration of transportation costs. Neither of these conditions holds in contemporary IB practice that is characterized by powerful multinational players and a global logistics network. Moreover, the Heckscher-Ohlin model is based upon the premise that both capital and labour are mobile domestically, but immobile between countries. In the modern business world, barriers to the movement of capital have been reduced and, with the advent of the Internet and electronic transactions, capital can be moved across the world in nanoseconds. While, at present, labour is not as internationally mobile as capital, people do migrate across the world for work – both now and long before Heckscher and Ohlin developed their theory. Finally, as with other theories discussed, the model assumes that free market competition and international exchange are good and beneficial for all within the involved nations. In the rest of this book, we will show how this assumption remains central to the model of globalization and IB that predominates at the present time, and perpetuates the principles of free trade and the ideology that the more open the market is for business, the greater the benefits to be accrued to all.

Critiques of classical and neo-classical trade theories

So far in this chapter we have sought to provide an overview of the early theories of international trade, since these constitute the conceptual underpinnings of contemporary IB. We have specifically engaged with the following theoretical developments: mercantilism, physiocratism, theory of absolute advantage, theory of comparative advantage, pure theory of trade, and theory of factor endowments. We have drawn attention to the links between early theoretical developments on international trade and the broader historical, political, social and economic contexts in which they took place. In particular, we have highlighted the central role of European nation states as the dominant actors in international political economy. These nation states sought to maximize their wealth, first, through accumulation of precious metals and, later, through trade exchange with other countries. The ideas of the mercantilists and, subsequently, of Adam Smith and other proponents of free markets and unrestrained trade provided an appealing theoretical justification for the realization of these objectives. They also legitimized the expansionist aspirations of European powers in terms of a projected increase in wealth and other benefits for all, across all involved countries. The betterment provided by these benefits was, however, relative to the individual's previous state and the existence and perpetuation of inequalities between groups was seen not only as unproblematic but also as necessary.

Classical theories of international trade, with their assumptions of the desirability of exchange and the accumulation of wealth, coincided with and underpinned the growth of capitalism as the dominant economic system. In contrast to medieval feudalism, in which ownership of land was the major indicator of wealth, for the new merchant classes that emerged as the implementers and beneficiaries of international trade, the key measure of wealth became ownership of financial capital and of the means of production. Over time, the central tenet of capitalism has been the need for growth; this was to be sustained by geographic expansion through the processes of colonization and imperialism. The colonization process was made possible through developments in technology and logistics, but it was driven primarily by government aspirations and actions. While the history of, say, the British Empire is generally written as one of heroic discovery, civilization and progress, critical commentators and postcolonial scholars provide accounts of endemic violence, exploitation and the ignoring of many generations of indigenous culture and civilization. They point to the continuing legacy of this hegemony in contemporary theories of business, management and organization.

The classical and neo-classical approaches to international trade are typically presented and summarized in terms of the rhetoric of growth and benefit. There is little or no mention of alternative views on economics in general and international exchange in particular, such as Marxism and its argumentation against the supposed ubiquitous social benefits of capitalism. However, consideration of theoretical alternatives to classical and neo-classical economics is necessary to create space for a critique of IB through references to empirical examples.

In this context, Marx's work is of particular significance. It originates from the first half of the nineteenth century, the period when free market economics dominated trade theory development. Moreover, Marx's ideas have underpinned much of the later critical thinking on political economy and society. In the next section, we provide a brief background to the ideas of Marx and a few other writers from the Marxist tradition, including Hobson, Lenin and Bukharin. The Marxist perspective draws attention to the fact that free market policies create conditions in which the monopolistic tendencies of capitalist enterprises can be realized. In addition, it highlights that not every party wins in trade exchange. At the level of international economy, it shows that some nations will derive benefits and others will be exploited. The same phenomenon can be observed at the country level, where some in society will increase their wealth at the expense of others.

The Marxist response

Karl Marx was one of the major critics of the social, political and economic structures of capitalism. For Marx, the growth of international trade was a key element in the development of capitalism and the emergence of the new class of affluent beneficiaries of industrialization – the 'bourgeoisie'. While Smith argued for increasing production and trade of commodities for the benefit of all in society, Marx (with Friedrich Engels) saw trade as the vehicle for accumulation of capital by the bourgeoisie through the exploitation of the working class. Marx and Engels (1848/2002) did not see the internationalization of production and exchange in terms of their aggregate outputs of increased production and consumption efficiency, but rather as manifestations of power in society. They, as well as later Marxist writers, associated the development of international trade with imperialism and colonization, and questioned the assumption that this trade is an inherently desirable project. Following Marx, in his book *Imperialism*, John Hobson (1902/1938) proposed that Britain's drive to develop its Empire did not result in increased wealth and improvement for the majority of its population. Contrary to perceived wisdom on the benefits of trade with its Empire, Hobson argued that the overall social and economic costs of imperialism far outweighed any advantages, even within Britain itself. On the basis of this assertion, Hobson (1902/1938: 46) asked the question, 'How is the British nation induced to embark upon such unsound business?' In response, he himself offered the following explanation: 'The only possible answer is that the business interests of the nation as a whole are subordinated to those of certain sectional interests that usurp control of the national resources and use them for their private gain' (ibid.). The sectional interests that he identified were those of the educated middle and upper classes with appropriate skills and resources, but with the primary role being that of the financial investors.

Hobson countered classical economic theories' assertions of benefit for all in society through trade by highlighting increased social and economic stratification. In a similar vein, Vladimir Ilich Lenin (1902/1969) argued that, rather than taking place under conditions of perfect competition, internationalization of production inevitably leads to the emergence of monopolies and inequality of power, characterized by the privileged position of the bourgeoisie over the working class. As organizations grow and develop home market monopolies, prospects for the generation of profits in this domestic market decrease. In search of new opportunities, geographic expansion takes place through colonization and the exploitation of resources in the colonized territories. In this way, surplus capital from the saturated domestic market is invested in order to create further economic growth and returns for the privileged few.

In contrast to the assumptions of classical and neo-classical theories – that international trade is a process of mutual benefit between nations – Lenin's argument points to it being one of exploitation of the colonized nations. The colonizers are seen as gaining advantage both from the importation of commodities from the colonies and from their investment in new infrastructure and development projects in them. Here, the productive resources of the colonies are appropriated by and absorbed into the capitalist enterprises of the colonizing nation. As such, for Lenin, international trade is first and foremost driven by the interests of capitalists and primarily benefits them. Lenin predicted that the increasing fragmentation and stratification of society would lead to growing conflict and to revolution and the overthrow of capitalism. Building upon Lenin's ideas, the topic of international trade was addressed by Nikolai Bukharin (1917/1987) in relation to the international division of labour. According to Bukharin, this international division would lead to the development of strong links between both capitalists and workers across national boundaries. While we might argue that the former is evident in contemporary society, with the rise of MNCs and the mobility of the wealthy as members of a new global elite, we would posit that there are at present few signs of effective cross-border organization of the labour movement.

Conclusion

In this chapter, we have placed our discussion of the historical antecedents of IB into a broader theoretical context. We have highlighted problematic aspects of international trade and IB that can be identified as inherent in both historical and contemporary practices. We have shown how, historically, the liberalization of trade did not necessarily proceed in a peaceful manner, based on all parties' understanding that it would bring benefits for all, but that coercion through military action had an important role to play in its spread. In order to understand how the conditions in which contemporary IB practices take place developed, it is necessary to be aware of the classical and neo-classical theories of international trade. If we are to critically appraise these theories and the impact of practices legitimized by them at a societal level, it is essential to have an understanding of the historical context in which these theories were built. In conclusion, we have seen the need for an acquaintance with alternative theories that challenge the underpinning logic of classical and neo-classical economics, and the circumstances in which the doctrine of free trade was implemented as the principle of trade between countries.

Questions

1. In what ways do classical theories of international trade explain and legitimize the ways in which international trade developed at the time of European geographical expansion?
2. From an historical perspective, what positive and negative consequences has the paradigm of 'free trade' had on the development of countries and regions across the world?
3. What insights into the emergence of economic inequalities between groups in society emerge from Marxist views on the effects of capitalism?

Further reading

Marx, K. (1890/2002) 'Commodities and money: Exchange process', *Das Kapital, Volume 1*. Salt Lake City, UT: University of Utah. pp. 170–196. Available at: http://content.csbs.utah.edu/~ehrbar/cap1.pdf (accessed 20 September 2016).

Smith, A. (1776/2007) *An Inquiry into the Nature and Causes of the Wealth of Nations*. Amsterdam: Meta Libri. pp. 47–54 (Chapter 7). Available at: www.ibiblio.org/ml/libri/s/SmithA_WealthNations_p.pdf (accessed 20 September 2016).

Young, R.J.C. (2003) *Postcolonialism: A Very Short Introduction*. Oxford: Oxford University Press.

2

Twentieth Century Developments in Trade and Investment Theories

Introduction

In this chapter, we consider the development of more recent theories of international business in the twentieth century, and their relationship to emerging forms of IB practice. The key change of focus that occurred in thinking about IB was a move from nation states as the key actors in IB to the emergence of the firm as the central player. As we will discuss, these theories address the subject of how to generate maximum profits for the company and its shareholders. We consider how, in so doing, they subordinate the interests of other stakeholders to those of the firm. We illustrate how, for example, issues of differential earning power across nations are viewed not as problematic, but as offering new sources of competitive advantage to the MNC.

The specific frameworks that we outline and provide a critical commentary on are: preference similarity theory; product life cycle theory; the Uppsala model of internationalization; new trade theory; strategic trade theory; and the model of the competitive advantage of nations. We then address issues of international investment, with an emphasis on foreign direct investment, portfolio investment and the nature of contemporary global financial markets.

The changing environment of international business

Towards the end of the nineteenth century, a lengthy phase of continuous growth in world trade was followed by economic slowdown and a decline in trade activity. In response to the changing economic climate and to pressures from internal producers, countries introduced punitive tariffs on imported commodities. For example, to protect the livelihood of their farmers, European governments closed their markets to imports of grain from Ukraine and the USA. Similarly, German Chancellor Otto Bismarck introduced tariffs in response to demands from landowners and industrialists, whilst in France the punitive Méline Tariff was imposed on imports. Having been slow to open its markets, the United States became one of the most protectionist nations, providing a cushion for its infant manufacturing industries as the country sought to recover from the economic impact of the Civil War.

Early in the twentieth century, this economic decline was brought to a temporary halt by the outbreak of the First World War, which stimulated growth and investment – primarily in the manufacture of instruments of war and in technological development of new weapons systems. After the First World War and a phase of growth in the 1920s, the course of economic decline resumed and culminated in the Great Depression that started in 1929 and continued for most of the 1930s. Throughout this period, governments across the world engaged in a new round of protectionist interventions and the imposition of tariffs and quotas. During the 1930s, the level of international trade dropped by between 20% and 38% for individual nations and by 1950 trade, as a share of national output, was at a lower level than it had been prior to the First World War.

Our overview of history shows that, at a theoretical level, policies of free trade have been advocated since the time of Adam Smith. It also demonstrates that in almost two centuries, these had not found a place on the official agenda of most governments. Likewise, international business nowadays does not operate in a free market context. To appreciate the extent of contemporary constraints within IB, it is necessary to move beyond focusing on the role of governments in shaping the global business environment, and to consider the significance and impact of companies in the development of more recent theories of IB. This has been reflected in the advancement of 'firm-based' theories that attempt to explain the nature of trade patterns across the world, and draw attention to the role of the demand side in explaining international trade patterns.

▬▬▬ Preference similarity theory

One of the first theories that considered the importance of both firms and the demand side for an understanding of trade exchange between countries was developed by Steffan Linder (1961) and is referred to as 'preference similarity theory' (Hufbauer, 1970). In his *Essay on Trade and Transformation*, Linder challenged Heckscher and Ohlin's focus on factors of production as the key determinants of exchange between nations. Seeking to explain trading patterns and partnerships – in particular, in relation to similar goods and between countries at a comparable level of economic development – Linder argued that actual trade depends upon factors that strengthen it, the so-called 'trade-creating forces', and those that hinder it, 'trade-braking forces'. He believed that the development of international trade arose from strengths in domestic demand and production, whereby a country would export those commodities for which it already had a strong home market. From this, he argued that the major trade-creating forces would be grounded in similarities of demand, based upon per capita income and consumer preferences, as determined by both economic and non-economic factors.

The trade-braking factors, on the other hand, were specified by Linder as being caused by the use of scarce factors in the demanded goods, physical distance or barriers to trade erected by governments. The implications of Linder's theory are that consumers in countries with a comparable level of income and with similar culture, climate, etc. will purchase similar goods, irrespective of whether or not they are made in their homeland. Following Linder's explanation of the underlying logic of intra-industry trade, and barring any trade-braking factors, a consumer in Germany, for example, will consider buying red wine from the Bordeaux, Chianti, Rheinhessen or Rioja regions and so, wine producers in France, Italy, Germany and Spain will all have access to the German market.

Various empirical studies have been undertaken to test Linder's theory. Some studies have supported Linder's proposition and have extended it beyond his original claim that it applied only to high-income countries, presenting evidence for its application to trade between 'less developed countries' (LDCs). Other writers, however, have questioned the strength of the trade-creating factors, and have pointed to the importance of geographical proximity as a major determinant of trade patterns. Issues of empirical accuracy notwithstanding, Linder's theory is mainly concerned with attempting to answer the question of which countries a firm can and should sell its products in, rather than with exploring whether and under what circumstances international business activities of companies are beneficial for society as a whole.

Product life cycle theory

Raymond Vernon (1966) proposed 'product life cycle theory' that describes three stages: from new product development, into maturity, and from there to standardization. At the development stage, a new product is produced and exported by the country in which it has originated through research and development (R&D). As it becomes accepted into the international marketplace, production is started up in other countries to meet the new demand. Subsequently, manufacture becomes concentrated in areas of greatest efficiency, so that the commodity ends up being exported back into the country where it was first conceived. Vernon's theory has been used to explain how the initial invention, technological development and production of many electronic goods was undertaken in Europe or the United States, and how gradually western countries moved from being producers and exporters of these goods, to becoming importers from LDCs which had taken on the manufacturing and exporting role.

Describing this technology transfer from country to country, Vernon's model implied that all countries have the opportunity to benefit from any innovation, regardless of where it originated. However, while Vernon admits that the innovation process generally begins in advanced economies, he does not engage with the fact that, as a consequence of this, these countries will derive maximum benefit from the early-stage, higher profits, thereby adding to their wealth. With increased production and its spread out into the LDCs, both the unit cost of production and profit levels decline markedly. As a result, the poorer countries derive a much lesser return from their involvement in the spread of the original innovation.

Critics argue that successful exploitation and wealth maximization from one innovation enables the already rich countries to accumulate both the financial and intellectual capital to fund further cycles of R&D and new product development, and hence, to generate above-average profits. LDCs, however, remain bound to the low-profit, mass-production stage. While this allows them to participate in industrialization, it does not enable them to increase their level of economic development to match developed countries. This contributes to ever-greater economic stratification at a global level and to the perpetuation of the 'north–south' divide. These extremes of innovation/production separation are manifest in the proliferation of low-cost manufacturing, especially in export processing zones (EPZs) and other tax- and regulation-free facilities.

The Uppsala model of internationalization

Johanson and Vahlne (1977) put forward a model attempting to explain the pattern of internationalization they observed based on the practices of Swedish companies in international markets. They discussed how companies draw upon experiential knowledge as they gradually expand their activities geographically and increase their commitment in terms of the type of international operations they engage in. Key to Johanson and Vahlne's (1977) model, commonly referred as the Uppsala model of internationalization, are the concepts of the 'establishment chain' and 'psychic distance'. The former refers to the incremental path of increased immersion in international markets, whereby companies begin with ad hoc exporting, followed by developing exports via intermediaries, before establishing their own sales and finally manufacturing operations in the host country. The latter refers to factors that pose obstacles to the understanding of foreign environments, such as cultural and linguistic differences, or variations in the institutional environment between home and host country. The model views firm internationalization as a dynamic process in which organizational learning, stemming from experience gained in a particular market and with a particular way of operating within it, plays a key role in the company's decisions about moving up the 'establishment chain' and entering markets characterized by a higher psychic distance than those with which the organization is already familiar. Obviously, internationalization activities develop down this trajectory as long as there are good prospects of performance for the company. The Uppsala model has over the years become a 'classic' framework for understanding internationalization from a behavioural rather than an economic perspective.

More recently, Johanson and Vahlne (2009) have revised their original model to include consideration of the significance of business networks in decision making on how and where to internationalize. Importantly, the authors claim that existing relationships and networks are of high relevance to decisions about which countries to target and the selected mode of entry. In this 'business network model', the establishment chain of the Uppsala model is seen as less valid as, in practice, firms do not necessarily proceed through all the available market entry modes on the continuum of low to high commitment. IB scholars now recognize that some firms are established with a view to being international from the outset – a process described as being 'born global'. Johanson and Vahlne (2009) have challenged this term contending that, in reality, these organizations are 'born regional' with a limited initial global profile.

Theories and terms such as the Uppsala model, business network model and the concepts of 'born global' or 'born regional' are useful in explaining the practices of IB organizations as observed by researchers. In this sense, they help in developing an understanding of companies' behaviour at a given point in time. In the contemporary international business context, the notion of the business network can be particularly helpful for understanding internationalization decisions and practices. This is especially the case when the network model is extended to incorporate the full range of stakeholders, including, for example, key customers, other businesses and government representatives in the host country.

New trade theory

The firm-based theories that we have discussed so far assume that the organization is working in a perfectly competitive market. The incorporation of 'imperfect' competitive conditions into models of trade was developed by Paul Krugman (1979, 1981) in his 'new trade theory'. Krugman pointed out that, even within competitive markets with a high number of different players, some firms will have an influence over the industry price structures. These companies will have grown faster than their competitors and achieved economies of scale, generating a degree of monopoly power within the market, and with it the potential to earn monopoly profits. These possibilities present an attractive proposition for new market entrants – including international ones – and, as such, might lead to increased competitive rivalry. To minimize the threat to their own business from both new and existing competitors, firms will develop specialization within a given product range. Where such specialization is undertaken by a number of companies from different countries, there will be an overall increase in the types of similar but differentiated products offered. As a result, consumers in all countries will have access to a wider choice of goods produced by firms in the same industry, and there will be growth in intra-industry trade between countries.

Krugman's major contribution to the theory of trade was to move away from the assumption of perfect competition, and to incorporate the notion of economies of scale as a factor motivating firms to engage in producing goods not only for domestic but also for international markets. Krugman's theory can be used to explain the case of Boeing and Airbus, both of which have grown through merger and acquisition and by establishing dominance in their home markets, but now compete against each other at a global level, including within each other's domestic market. However, Krugman's model excludes the influence of a number of factors – such as geographical distance, the role of government and the existence of trade blocs – upon overall trade patterns. The significance of one such factor – the role of government – is specifically addressed in 'strategic trade theory', which explores the possible range of impacts of government intervention under the circumstances of imperfect competition.

Krugman's theory suggests that firms will seek to grow internationally to take advantage of economies of scale and to win market share from their competitors. It addresses the question of what a firm would consider as 'good' from the point of view of profit generation. However, it does not problematize the way in which this drive towards geographic expansion and achievement of a monopoly position impacts other stakeholders.

Competitive advantage of nations

Michael Porter contributed a key model to understanding aspects of IB relating to choice of business location. This model, that addresses *The Competitive Advantage of Nations* (Porter, 1990), is referred to as 'Porter's Diamond'. The diamond incorporates four country-specific attributes that shape the business environment, making countries more or less attractive as targets of business activity. These are: (1) factor endowments; (2) demand conditions; (3) related and supporting industries; and (4) business strategy, structure and rivalry.

The first of these refers to a country's productive capabilities, such as its pool of skilled labour, its natural resources and its infrastructure. The workforce may constitute a source of competitive advantage both in terms of the available skill levels, and in relation to the cost of employment. Some countries are seen as attractive locations for establishing operations, being able to offer a supply of cheap labour, coupled with other factors that are favourable to the investing company. This logic, however, which legitimizes the search for ever-cheaper production costs and the organizational practice of moving operations accordingly has been criticized as generating a 'race to the bottom'.

The second attribute in Porter's diamond describes the quality and quantity of demand for a given type of product in companies' home markets. According to Porter, the relative strength of demand and the discerning nature of consumers gives firms the competitive edge that then enables them to compete successfully in international markets. For Porter, it is not the size of the market, but the crucial element of 'character' that is important. The third attribute addresses how all organizations are parts of networks in which they rely upon other firms to supply them with components, raw materials, or different types of support services. The presence and international competitiveness of these supplementary organizations will be a key factor when the firm is assessing possible business locations. Nowadays, MNCs establish global networks of suppliers based upon their ability to provide relevant capabilities on the most advantageous business terms. Porter's fourth attribute relates to the organization's fit with, and flexibility in adapting to, prevailing business conditions in its home market over time. Porter highlights that there is no universal formula for business strategy. Rather, successful firms need to be willing and able to change in order to remain competitive within a dynamic business environment.

In addition to these four attributes, Porter identifies two impacting variables: chance and government-related factors. Chance encapsulates those major events or innovations that have not been foreseen and that have the capability of driving a fundamental reshaping of an industry. The intervention of government can come in a variety of forms, generated through legislation and policy. Examples include changes in tax structures and subsidies offered to businesses and the elevation of some countries to the status of 'most favoured nations'.

Critique of Porter's framework

Porter's model brings together elements of both country- and firm-based theories of international trade. While there is consideration of country-specific factor endowments and their influence on trade flows, Porter sees firms as the key players in contemporary IB. The role of countries lies in the creation of an environment that either helps or hinders the extent to which firms are able to compete internationally. For Porter, the major driver of firm performance is the search for competitive advantage that will result in the generation of above-average profits and, hence, the highest return to financial shareholders. Porter acknowledges that the possibilities for the global configuration of value-adding activities are underpinned by structural discrepancies across countries. These may take the form of earning differentials between societies, with recognition of the benefits firms can derive from countries offering low-cost labour. In mass-market consumer economies, this enables firms to increase the range of product offerings, at the same time constantly reducing the real cost of these to the consumer. Variations in the cost of infrastructure provisions – buildings, roads, ports and power – provide further advantages to business. Also, differences in governmental regulatory frameworks, stipulating levels of tax and duty, environmental and labour laws, and degrees of intervention or *laissez-faire*, become central to decision making.

Porter sees firms as operating within a given external environment, without obligation to influence it for the benefit of others. In his analysis, economic, social, technological and legislative differentials between countries are seen as opportunities for companies and their customers, rather than as global societal issues. This approach accords with the previously mentioned maxim of the economist Milton Friedman (1962) to the effect that any business has but one social responsibility: to maximize the return on investment for its financial stakeholders through the most effective allocation of resources, as long as this is done fairly and competitively and within the legal frameworks that prevail. However, Friedman himself recognized that this view of firms' responsibilities left unanswered the questions 'Who protects the consumer?' and 'Who protects the worker?' (Friedman and Friedman, 1980).

Dependency theory

There are alternative discourses that challenge theoretical developments that focus on the generation of profit and shareholder value, without explicit consideration of impacts on broader society and with an implicit assumption that free markets will in the end benefit all. These include a body of social theories under the umbrella title 'dependency theory', the roots of which lie in the work of the Economic Commission for Latin America (ECLA). ECLA emerged in the 1950s, led by the economist Raúl Prebisch (see Prebisch, 1971). The group identified a trend of deterioration in the terms of trade between Latin American countries and their richer trade partners in the north. This trend, they argued, commenced in the era of sixteenth-century colonialism and, over the centuries, resulted in a continuous decline in the wealth of poor nations as that of rich nations grew.

According to the theory, dependency is maintained through a series of mechanisms, ranging from political and economic policies, to exploitation of cheap natural and labour resources, cultural and intellectual hegemony, and the passing on of obsolete technologies. Moreover, dependency theorists point to the role of elites in the poor nations in maintaining the state of dependency and underdevelopment, through acting as enablers of – and being profiteers from – the activities of developed world MNCs and financial institutions. Dependency theory spread and influenced scholars in the north, particularly neo-Marxists such as Andre Frank (1978). The relationship between rich and poor countries was also explored by Baran (1957), who considered the causes of some countries' 'underdevelopment' and linked these to the accumulation of the wealth derived from their natural and labour resources by the developed countries. Responses given by dependency theorists to the exploitative economic relationships they describe vary. Some, like Frank, do not see the possibility of escape within the capitalist system. Others, such as Cardoso (1972), consider that countries can seek to adjust the system to their benefit. Dependency theory is also drawn upon by authors from the 'world systems theory' school, to which we refer later in this chapter.

Investment theories of IB

The literature distinguishes between two main types of international investment, with the criterion for the distinction being the question of control (see Hymer, 1960/1976). The first, where foreign assets are acquired with the objective of taking control over them, is referred to as 'foreign direct investment' (FDI). In contrast, the second type is focused on a purely financial interest, without a drive for control. This activity centres on purchases of shares, government bonds or other financial assets, and is classified as 'portfolio investment'. Contemporarily, portfolio investment takes place at the level of a global network of exchanges, for example, where pension funds seek to maximize the return on their members' investments by dealing in shares across the world's stock markets.

International investment funding can come from a number of sources, including transnational agencies such as the IMF or World Bank, commercial banks and country governments. It may also take several different forms, ranging from equity transfer, where the investor takes a stake in the host country market, to debt investment, where the investor retains the original value of the capital transfer, plus interest due. While the first exposes the investor to risk, in the latter case, other than in the case of government default or institutional bankruptcy, the investor is not exposed in this way. In addition to types of investment involving capital transfer, there exist 'non-equity' investment types: licensing, franchising, alliances and sub-contracting.

Foreign direct investment

In the past, FDI was mainly a one-way process, constituting one of the economic aspects of European imperialism and colonization of new territories. Now, however, FDI investments take place at a global level within complex networks. For example, the global automotive industry has seen FDI from Japan and Europe to the United States, from Europe to Japan and Central America, from the USA to Europe and China, and from China, India, South Korea and Malaysia to Europe. FDI can be divided into a number of sub-categories, based upon different criteria. One such categorization differentiates between 'greenfield' and 'merger and acquisition' (M&A) investments. Greenfield investment is centred on the setting up of a completely new operation in the host country, whereas M&A investment involves the home country firm in either joining with or purchasing an existing company in the host country.

Another classification of types of FDI introduces the distinction between 'horizontal FDI' and 'vertical FDI'. Horizontal FDI refers to activity whereby an organization invests in a business that operates in the same industry as itself. In addition to being set in an intra-industry context, horizontal FDI has historically taken place between companies headquartered in developed countries. However, more recently, MNCs from emerging economies have engaged in FDI in developed economies, such as India's Tata Motors' purchase of Jaguar Land Rover from Ford.

In contrast to horizontal FDI, vertical FDI may be inter-industry, whereby one organization seeks to procure sources of materials or components for its own products, or support services that underpin its market offerings. Vertical FDI is often set in the context of developed-to-developing economy investment, whereby the home company seeks to drive down the cost of doing business by exploiting lower-wage operations in the host country. An example of vertical FDI is the investment by Anglophone nations' service industries in call centres in India, in order to deliver customer support on a lower cost basis than in the home country.

The distinction between horizontal and vertical FDI has important implications for the FDI recipient countries, and for the overall discussion about the benefits of FDI. In the hope of encouraging economic advancement, many developing countries initiate policies to attract FDI, with the expectation that this will result in increased employment and technological spillover. However, these positive effects are more likely to occur in the case of horizontal, rather than vertical, FDI. Since vertical FDI often involves locating the production of technologically simple and low-skilled labour-intensive elements in countries that are abundant in low-skilled labour, it has a much lower potential for generating spillovers and linkages. Despite the problematic nature of the effects of FDI on the host country economy, both horizontal and vertical FDI are considered as advantageous by MNCs and, with increasing globalization of the economy, the importance of FDI continues to grow.

Whatever form FDI takes, production is based in the host country without the transfer of goods from the home operation. At the same time, financing is frequently undertaken by borrowing within the host country and, as such, need not involve any transfer of capital between countries. In addition, profits generated within the host country may be reinvested there, rather than being transferred back to the home country. Hymer (1960/1976) showed that FDI often builds into a complex set of relationships between nations that may involve a two-way flow of FDI, with no actual transfer of products or capital between them, and no reliance upon any overall advantageous economic or legal environment in one or other. Here, the FDI by both parties is entirely based upon borrowing within the respective host countries, delivery of the product or service within the host market, and reinvestment of profits generated also within the host nation.

Dunning's 'eclectic theory'

Broadening out from Hymer's FDI approach, further investment theories have been proposed. The most prolific writer on these is John Dunning (1977, 1980, 1981, 2000). Dunning developed a series of interpretations of drivers of the internationalization of business, identifying three sets of advantages that firms might seek to exploit, namely: ownership, location and internalization (OLI). The first of these relates to a set of advantages that are specific to the firm, its competitive advantage over its rivals and its ability to exploit investment opportunities. It is argued that a firm owning an asset that contributes to the creation of competitive advantage in the home market can exploit this advantage through entering foreign markets using FDI. Such assets may be either tangible or intangible, for example: financial capital, technologies, skilled labour, natural resources or intellectual capital. The second set is specific to a country: those structural features that attract inward investment. Location advantages may be derived, for example, from access to natural resources, the pool of available labour – whether manual or intellectual – or, as in the case of Singapore, from the country's position on global trade routes. The final set addresses why an organization might decide to internationalize through FDI rather than by other routes – for example, exporting, franchising or licensing. The internalization route is likely to be chosen by a firm where the transaction cost of pursuing one of these alternatives exceeds that of building its own international operations.

Dunning's 'eclectic theory' has been valuable because of its comprehensive treatment of a variety of factors governing foreign direct investment. At the same time, critics point to its shortcomings in this very respect. Dunning himself acknowledged that eclectic theory offers endless possibilities for examining motivations behind FDI, such that it can always be applied as an explanatory framework without fear of falsification. Beyond this critique at a theoretical level, there are contemporary IB practices that run counter to Dunning's propositions. While Dunning identifies advantages in ownership and internalization, since the 1980s, many MNCs have sought to build competitive advantage through processes of outsourcing and contracting, prioritizing production flexibility and the ability to source at the lowest possible cost over building longer-term embeddedness through ownership or internalization.

It is also worth noting that Dunning's approach addresses the topic of investment entirely from the investing company's point of view. It speaks about 'advantages' and 'costs' in relation to the internationalizing firm. However, it does not engage with the fact that FDI is not necessarily advantageous for the host country. As empirical examples suggest, it may result in driving local companies out of business, polluting the natural environment and depleting local natural resources, while generating few employment opportunities for local people and little or no tax revenue for the host government. We would argue for the need to approach the subject of FDI from the perspective of all affected parties.

Knowledge–capital model of FDI

Another theoretical framework that addresses the determinants of FDI location is Markusen's (1998) 'knowledge–capital' (KK) model. It incorporates consideration of the distinction between horizontal and vertical FDI to explain how domestic firms as well as vertically- or horizontally-integrated MNCs develop. Markusen's model is based upon three major assumed conditions that he labels: fragmentation, skilled-labour intensity and jointness. The first of these implies the possibility for the location of knowledge-based assets to be fragmented from those of production. It is assumed that the incremental cost of knowledge transfer to a foreign plant is small, relative to that of supplying a single domestic plant. The second condition is that the generation of these knowledge services is more skilled-labour intensive than is the production element. Finally, the notion of jointness relates to the ability to share knowledge-based assets across multiple production locations. It is important to distinguish between the first and third of these assumptions. An example of fragmentation is where a multinational oil company has a small team of seismographers based, say, in its home at Houston, Texas. It is more effective for the company to send the team to operate in different locations as required than to provide this specialist service across all individual country operations. However, the seismographic team can only operate in one location at any one time. In comparison, an example of jointness is seen where Microsoft centralizes software development in multiple locations, but can share the knowledge output from these across the world simultaneously.

According to the KK model, the implications of fragmentation and skilled-labour intensity are such that MNCs will engage in vertical FDI in different countries, depending upon factor prices and market sizes. On the other hand, the occurrence of jointness will give rise to MNCs investing horizontally, that is, generating outputs in a number of countries. Markusen's model links the emergence of vertical and horizontal FDI by MNCs to differences in country characteristics, such as size, factor endowments, costs of trade and investment costs.

Within the KK model there is an unstated assumption that the firm is the central actor in international investment, having agency to construct its global structures depending upon the various factors outlined above. As such, it is again seen as unproblematic that MNCs' exploitation of structural differences between countries for the benefit of their own production and process efficiency and profit maximization is likely to be at the expense of resource exploitation and depletion, environmental degradation and increasing socio-economic fragmentation.

Portfolio investment

While FDI has been the focus of much discussion of international investment, it is not necessary that the key objective of such investment will be ownership of or control over a company or any physical asset. Portfolio investment is directed towards the acquisition of 'paper assets' in another country. These may take the form of, for example, equities or bonds. The first of these, that might involve a shareholding in a foreign company without control or ownership, is a form of equity investment, where the investor shares in the risk that the value of the investment may fall, rather than increase. The second is a form of debt transfer, where the face value of the bond (i.e. of the initial capital investment in whatever agreed currency) is maintained and interest is due on the investment. As explained above, except in circumstances of default by or bankruptcy of the bond issuer, the bond holder carries no share of risks.

The importance of portfolio investments increased greatly in the early 1990s, with the easing of international exchange controls and growth in the amount of developed country capital seeking high rates of return at a time of low interest rates in the home economies. During this time, cross-border capital flows grew to exceed the amount of international trade flows. That is to say, 'paper investments' became more important than those in 'real' entities, such as companies or physical assets. For a period, the world economy supported growth and return on portfolio investments, largely through the rapid development of the economies of South East Asia and Russia, with their demand for goods and services in their home markets and their strong export performance to developed economies. This prompted an influx of external capital from investors seeking above average returns on the capital invested. However, this growth rate proved unsustainable and, following on from the collapse of the Thai economy in 1997, the subsequent 'Asian financial crisis' had global repercussions. A decade later, and with more devastating and long-lasting impact, the global financial crisis, which began with the USA sub-prime mortgage crisis and spread across the world's financial institutions and economies, demonstrated the interconnectedness, complexity and lack of transparency of global portfolio investment flows.

Beyond the centrality of nations and firms

Many writers on FDI base their ideas upon the notion that the capitalist firm is the main actor in IB, and that it legitimately seeks to maximize its profits by achieving production efficiency through FDI. This view is in line with those that underpin classical theories of international trade, as first put forward by Smith, Torrens and Ricardo. These theories, as explained in Chapter 1, proposed that countries should specialize in the production of those goods that they are able to manufacture most efficiently. Viewed from this perspective, contemporary FDI – through the activities of MNCs – can be considered as contributing to the attainment of the most efficient distribution and configuration of production at a global level. It is this rationale that is adopted by those who justify the current processes of globalization of industries. However, Smith's and others' argumentation was firmly rooted in the concept of a free market and in the belief that such a free market would ultimately lead to the accumulation of wealth for all nations, to the benefit of all citizens relative to their own previous situation.

The assumptions that underpin these theories are problematic in a number of ways. At a theoretical level, they can be challenged by Marxist political and economic theory that, rather than viewing MNCs as facilitators of wealth generation for all, sees them as instruments of exploitation and appropriation of resources to the sole benefit of their home country shareholders. Arguably, the enhanced potential for mobility of location for firms from rich countries inherent in FDI under free market economic conditions leads to a weakened position for workers in the home country in wage or employment negotiations. Similarly, it puts workers in the host country in a situation of uncertainty of employment, stemming from the possibility that the foreign investment may be withdrawn.

While the analysis of world trade offered by dependency theory, referred to earlier, distinguishes between 'core' and 'periphery', 'world systems theory' (see Wallerstein, 1974, 2004) argues that the global economic system is characterized by a division of labour between three zones: core, semi-periphery and periphery. In this model, which is defined in terms of power relations – political, economic and military – the nations at the core are those that exercise dominance over others, but are not themselves dominated. Those at the periphery, on the other hand, are subject to domination, but hold no power over others. The middle category consists of those countries that are both exploiters of others, at the periphery, but are themselves exploited by the core. Although they gain advantage from their exploitation through accruing some of the benefits of world economic activity, they lack military power that would allow them to take control over redistribution of economic output. This group is seen as essential for the smooth operation of the world capitalist system, that otherwise would be polarized and, hence, less politically stable.

As far as specific types of economic activity within the world system are concerned, companies from the core and the semi-periphery are in a privileged position compared to those at the periphery. With the support of their home governments, they are able to secure control over the most profitable activities within the international division of labour, generating high profits for themselves and contributing to the perpetuation of a situation of inequality. Within a hierarchical ordering, the countries of the core maintain their control over the semi-periphery, and the semi-periphery over periphery. Viewed through the lens of world systems theory, FDI is seen by some as not constituting a politically neutral activity of a purely economic nature. Rather, it is considered as an instrument of control used by powerful nations to dominate the less powerful ones.

The political dimension of FDI is also evident when discussion of foreign investment and its impacts takes place from a postcolonial perspective. Through adopting this approach, it can be argued that MNCs and the institutions of FDI have a vested interest in perpetuating historical differences in levels of economic, social and technological development in order to maintain the home country entities' domination over host country factors of production. As some commentators point out, these types of activity by MNCs, governments and other IB actors are symptomatic of an inherent problem of IB: that it is and always will be dominated by powerful actors who will dictate the rules of the game and what constitutes freedom within it.

Conclusion

In this chapter, we have expanded our discussion of theoretical developments in IB, specifically pointing to the move from country- to firm-based frameworks. In particular, we have highlighted the centrality of the idea of profit maximization for MNCs within more recent IB theories. Further, through a critical discussion of international investment theories, we have considered the implications of FDI and other forms of investment for different stakeholders and the overall global financial system. Finally, in introducing dependency-based theories, we have offered an alternative view of the outcomes of IB activity for both developed and developing economies.

To this point, we have aimed to offer an understanding of how thinking about IB as both an intellectual and a practical domain has been rooted in specific political, economic, social and technological contexts. The particular way in which IB has evolved, as well as its current status, has not been a purely 'natural' process, in the sense of having been determined by market forces operating under the conditions of perfect competition. Rather, it has been influenced by certain actors in pursuit of their interests at different points in time. It has also been strongly connected to the development of capitalism as the prevalent economic system in Europe, and to its spread across the world.

Questions

1. What are the impacts of international investment activity upon the economies of developing countries under conditions of profit maximization and shareholder return for the MNC?
2. Who are the 'winners' and 'losers' in both developed and developing nations under these conditions?
3. What are your views regarding the future consequences of international investment for broader society and the environment if these conditions prevail?

Further reading

Davies, R.B. and Vadlamannati, K.C. (2013) 'A race to the bottom in labor standards? An empirical investigation', *Journal of Development Economics*, 103: 1–14. Summarized in *The Economist*, 27 November 2013. Available at: www.economist.com/blogs/freeexchange/2013/11/labour-standards (accessed 22 September 2016).

Markusen, J.R. and Venables, A.J. (1998) 'Multinational firms and the new trade theory', *Journal of International Economics*, 46: 183–203. Available at: www.princeton.edu/~erossi/courses_files/Markusen.pdf (accessed 21 September 2016).

Re-Define (undated) *Foreign Direct Investment – A Critical Perspective*, a Re-Define Working Paper. Available at: http://re-define.org/sites/default/files/ForeignDirectInvestment-Acriticalper.pdf (accessed 22 September 2016).

3

Institutions of International Business

▰▰▰▰ Introduction

In the first two chapters, we presented an overview of international business from an historical perspective. We drew attention to the shift in focus of international trade and IB from being country to firm-based. Here, we discuss the contemporary institutional frameworks underpinning IB and, in so doing, outline the various factors that contributed to their emergence and development over time. An awareness of at least some aspects of the political and economic conditions that prevailed at different times in the nineteenth and twentieth centuries is essential for an understanding of the present role and status of key institutions like the International Monetary Fund (IMF), the World Bank and the World Trade Organization (WTO). It is also helpful in comprehending the growth of new structures of economic cooperation and integration between countries, such as the Association of South East Asian Nations (ASEAN) and the Common Market of the South (MERCOSUR). In engaging with various views regarding the implications of these institutions for different actors, we develop a discussion in which they are seen as being both key to the solution and part of the problem of trade imbalance and economic inequalities at a global level.

▰▰▰▰ The international monetary system

For many centuries, trade that was not based upon barter (i.e. exchange of goods) was most often undertaken using gold coins as the means of payment. However, with the development and growth of international trade from the nineteenth century on, it became impractical to use gold as the payment medium as, for example, in transporting a shipload of gold from London to Hong Kong in order to pay for a consignment of China tea. In changing to a system of currency-based trade exchange, between 1870 and 1914 the main players in international trade adopted a 'gold standard' system, whereby the value of their individual currencies was 'pegged' to that of gold. Each currency had a defined conversion rate in relation to the weight of gold for which it could be exchanged and countries could then value their own currency in relation to any other using this common yardstick. The emergence of the gold standard was paralleled by the economic and colonial domination of the United Kingdom, in an era when it was said that 'the sun never sets on the British Empire'. During this period, the pound sterling was the strongest and most widely used currency in settling international transactions and London emerged as the major financial centre in the world.

With the outbreak of the First World War, countries withdrew from the gold standard and, despite efforts to reinstate it in the interwar years, it finally collapsed with the economic downturn of the Great Depression that began in October 1929. At that time, countries became more preoccupied with their internal economic problems than with engaging in international trade. In 1931, the Bank of England cut the link between the value of gold and that of sterling, allowing the pound to 'float' on international financial exchanges with its value determined by market forces. Until the outbreak of the Second World War, the lack of stability within the international monetary system had not been resolved. Towards the end of the War, in 1944 the Bretton Woods conference was held with the intention to provide a framework for global economic and social stability. One of the agreements reached was that the US dollar would be tied to the value of gold, and all other countries would peg their currencies to the dollar. Individual countries retained freedom to apply controls to the flow of private capital and they could only seek a revaluation of their currency where they found themselves in conditions of 'fundamental disequilibrium'.

The Bretton Woods system combined the objectives of trade liberalization with governments' desire to maintain a degree of control over their domestic economies. However, its lifespan was limited to less than 30 years and a number of factors contributed to its failure. First, from the 1950s, in parallel with the dollar-bound currency exchange system, 'euromarkets' emerged as a major attractor of foreign currency deposits in European banks. This Eurocurrency market was not subject to government capital controls and, as such, it grew rapidly, contributing to the increasing strength of European economies. On the other hand, throughout the 1960s, the US economy experienced rising inflation and a growing trade deficit. Also in the 1960s, members of the Organization of the Petroleum Exporting Countries (OPEC) started to exercise their economic power, significantly raising the price of oil and generating high levels of earnings that they subsequently invested in international money markets. The growing complexity of international financial flows, coupled with economic uncertainty around the world, led to a questioning of the ability of the signatories of the Bretton Woods agreement to fulfil their commitments. In 1971, the system finally collapsed when US President Richard Nixon announced the end of convertibility of the US dollar to gold.

A new framework establishing the rules governing the international monetary system was settled in January 1976, known as the Jamaica Agreement. This agreement stipulated that the value of world currencies would not be fixed, but that countries would be allowed to choose the exchange system that would be most suitable to their economic interests. Countries chose either to allow their currency to float or to be pegged in relation to that of another country. The examples of Hong Kong and the European Economic Community (EEC) are illustrative of the diversity of solutions adopted. Hong Kong has pegged the value of its dollar to that of the US dollar for over 30 years, maintaining this link beyond its transition from being a British colony to becoming a Special Administrative Region (SAR) of the People's Republic of China (PRC). As part of the European integration process, members of the EEC created the European Monetary System (EMS), within which most countries joined the 'exchange rate mechanism' (ERM). Under the ERM, individual currency exchange rates were fixed against one another within a range of +/– 2.25% of par value, at the same time maintaining a floating rate in relation to the US dollar and to other non-ERM currencies. The establishment of the EMS facilitated the introduction of the euro by a number of European countries, first as an accounting currency in 1999, then in the form of banknotes and coins in 2002. While, within the contemporary international monetary system both pegged and fixed exchange rate mechanisms are adopted, a number of leading economies, including the USA and Japan, employ an approach that permits their currency to float according to market forces, simultaneously allowing space for government intervention. This takes place through setting interest rates, taxation regimes and other domestic financial frameworks in order to influence the economic environment. However, many would argue that the international financial system is now so complex that individual countries have only limited influence over their currency's value on the exchanges.

Origins of the International Monetary Fund

As well as setting the post-Second World War international monetary system framework, the Bretton Woods conference saw the establishment of two of the supranational institutions that play a key role in the contemporary world of IB: the International Monetary Fund and the International Bank for Reconstruction and Development (IBRD), now commonly referred to as the World Bank. The underlying objective behind the creation of these two bodies was, in the words of the then US Treasury Secretary Henry Morgenthau, the 'creation of a dynamic world community in which the peoples of every nation will be able to realize their potentialities' (Bretton Woods Project, 2005). The IMF has grown from an original membership of less than 50 countries in 1945 to 188 nations in 2016. The stated purpose of the IMF is 'to foster global monetary cooperation, secure financial stability, facilitate international trade, promote high employment and sustainable economic growth, and reduce poverty around the world' (IMF, 2016). In addition, the IMF's task is to provide temporary financial support to countries that experience balance of trade and currency exchange difficulties. Financial assistance from the IMF is conditional upon the implementation of economic reforms that are designed to enable countries to address their balance of payments problems. The IMF stipulates specific structural adjustment policies (SAPs) for its borrowers and loans are issued in instalments only as these are put in place.

The IMF operates in three areas. First, it undertakes surveillance, both monitoring economic and financial developments and offering policy advice specifically aimed at crisis prevention. Second, it lends to countries experiencing balance of payments difficulties to provide temporary finance and, additionally, to put in place policies aimed at correcting the underlying problems. According to the IMF, loans to poorer countries are specifically directed towards poverty reduction. Third, the IMF offers technical assistance to countries to supply training in its areas of expertise. In support of these three areas, the IMF undertakes research and gathers economic statistics. In the wake of the emerging market crises of the 1990s and, subsequently, the GFC, the IMF (in conjunction with the World Bank) has worked to increase its effectiveness in preventing and resolving crises through developing standards and codes of good practice in its areas of responsibility.

The IMF gains most of its funding from its members' 'quota subscriptions', the amounts of which are based upon the relative size of their economies. The size of the quota also determines the extent to which the individual member country can draw upon IMF support when required. More significantly, voting rights within the IMF are determined by the relative size of the quota and, as such, the USA as the largest subscriber holds the biggest bloc of votes.

Growth and development of the World Bank

The largest public development institution in the world, the World Bank is based in Washington, DC and has 188 member countries, with participation being contingent upon membership of the IMF. It was established with the purposes of 'assist(ing) in the reconstruction and development of territories of members by facilitating the investment of capital for productive purposes' and of 'promot[ing] the long-range balanced growth of international trade and the maintenance of equilibrium in balances of payments by encouraging international investment ... thereby assisting in raising the productivity, the standard of living and conditions of labour in their territories' (World Bank, 1989). The World Bank (2016) 'has set two goals for the world to achieve by 2030: end extreme poverty by decreasing the percentage of people living on less than $1.90 a day to no more than 3%; [and] promote shared prosperity by fostering the income growth of the bottom 40% for every country'. The term 'World Bank' is commonly used in joint reference to two specific institutions: the original IBRD, which was reconstituted as the lending arm of the bank to 'middle-income' countries (MICs), and the International Development Association (IDA), founded in 1960, which offers funds to the world's poorest nations.

Altogether, five institutions form what is referred to as the World Bank Group, namely, the original International Bank for Reconstruction and Development (IBRD), the IDA, the International Finance Corporation (IFC), the Multilateral Investment Guarantee Agency (MIGA) and the International Centre for Settlement of Investment Disputes (ICSID). In addition to the IBRD and IDA, the IFC offers loan and equity finance for private sector projects in developing countries. The role of the MIGA is to support foreign direct investment to developing countries through providing political risk insurance. The ICSID facilitates settlement of disputes between member governments and foreign investors in investment-related matters. The administration of the World Bank encompasses all five institutions, with a common Board of Governors led by the World Bank President. In order to obtain necessary loan funds, the Bank issues bonds and sells them on international capital markets. To ensure that the loans are repaid, the Bank (like the IMF) imposes conditions upon borrowing countries, typically involving social, structural and sectoral reforms. As with the IMF, the extent of the influence of an individual member country upon the World Bank's decision-making processes depends upon the amount of the member's capital subscription. As such, the USA holds almost 17% of the voting power, in comparison with just over 5% shared amongst the 48 member countries with the lowest subscription amounts.

Critiques of the IMF and the World Bank

As outlined above, the decision-making processes and voting rights within the IMF and World Bank are heavily influenced by individual member countries' financial contribution, which is determined by the size of their economies. The major locus of power lies within the leading industrialized countries, specifically the G7 group of nations (previously G8 until Russia's suspension from the group following its annexation of Crimea in 2014). The G7 comprises Canada, France, Germany, Italy, Japan, the UK and the USA. In 2014, the combined GDP of the G7 countries represented around 45% of the global economy. The G7 members are thereby in a position to dominate IMF and World Bank policies with little consultation with less developed nations.

Critics point to how these policies do not necessarily result in improvements to the social and economic conditions for those countries that are the subject of IMF and World Bank programmes. On the contrary, IMF policies have been seen as leading to a reduction in public access to basic services, an increase in the incidence of poverty and to economic contraction and recession. This is seen as stemming from the 'structural adjustment' terms upon which support is conditional. In many cases, these terms (often described as grounded in the neoliberal 'Washington consensus') emphasize the need for the liberalization of trade and investment in the country's financial sector as well as the privatization and deregulation of SOEs. Since recipient country governments are obliged to comply with the requirements of the IMF or World Bank structural adjustment programmes, criticisms have been expressed regarding the lack of consideration of local circumstances and, in addition, the potential removal of a country's ability to shape its own economic policies.

An example that vividly illustrates 'unhappy experiences' (Ito, 2012) with IMF loans refers to Thailand, Indonesia and Korea; countries that were subject to IMF programmes in the late 1990s in response to the Asian currency crisis. The economic problems that resulted from the imposed restructuring in these countries were manifold. They included: excessively tight fiscal and monetary policies that led to severe recession; too much conditionality on reforms, exemplified by bank restructuring and IMF-recommended bank closures that resulted in a banking crisis, further exacerbating the situation; the insufficient size of the loan package that adversely impacted the effectiveness of the assistance; and the perception of the borrowers that the assistance package was influenced by the interests of large firms and IMF shareholders, that resulted in many Asian policymakers feeling mistreated.

More recently, there has been criticism of the IMF, and reports of internal conflict, over lending to bail out the Greek economy. While the President and other European Directors drove the decision, allegedly to protect the rest of the eurozone economy, non-European members were highly sceptical. They pointed out that the loan was in breach of the IMF's own rules – that lending should not be given to countries that could not afford to pay their debts, and that it should be dependent on debt structural adjustment, allowing the nation to write off some of this debt. The latter was rejected by European governments, in fear of collapse of their own banks to which Greece was indebted. In mid-2015, Greece became the first advanced economy to default on an IMF loan. As we write this book, the country's economy continues to languish, with very high unemployment and underlying social unrest.

In relation to the World Bank, concerns have been expressed about the social and environmental consequences of some of the major infrastructure projects that it has supported. For example, the Bank has been subject to intense scrutiny over the conditions that prevail in some regions where it has funded so called 'development projects' (Human Rights Watch, 2015). In particular, it has been attacked for its support for hydroelectric dam projects in developing countries, where critics say that the social and environmental impacts on local communities and habitats outweigh the benefits to the countries. In Northern India there have been reports of regular threats and intimidation of local people protesting against a Bank-funded hydroelectric power project. The Bank's loan provisions include requirements for consultation with local communities and for oversight of human rights compliance. Despite numerous complaints about abuses to the World Bank and its representatives, no action had been taken in response to these. In one instance, it was claimed that after a World Bank Inspection Panel visit, the Panel's interpreter was imprisoned and a computer that might have contained identities of those who spoke to the Panel was seized by security forces. There have been similar reports relating to Bank-funded projects in numerous countries, including Cambodia, Chad and China.

The World Bank has also been criticized for its over-emphasis on the role of markets and private sector investment in fostering international development. This has been the case especially where the Bank has offered support for the delivery of education and healthcare by private suppliers who may replace the country's own public sector provision. In the education arena, World Bank policies aimed at poverty alleviation have been operationalized through expansion of privately provided schooling. While the institution – the largest individual source of finance for education in low-income countries – claims to make its policies and decisions based on the principle of bureaucratic neutrality guided by scientific expertise, the World Bank has been criticized for being a 'policy entrepreneur', acting to expand private provision in education. As Mundy and Menashy (2014) point out, the Bank has relied in its education-related policies on the ideologically biased recommendations of its own economists, rather than on the views of the Bank's education sector staff and the governments in developing countries.

In the field of healthcare, an example has been given of how the Bank's IFC institution has invested in a private healthcare partnership in Lesotho. Oxfam's (2014) report revealed that the project consumed 51% of the nation's healthcare budget, while the private company involved was taking in 25% returns. As another example, in Eastern Europe the IFC invested $5m in a Romanian private healthcare company. This is reported to have become a popular destination with international medical tourists who travel to the country for surgical and non-surgical treatments, including cosmetic procedures at a lower cost than in any other European country.

As the IMF and World Bank constitute major international players, not only in the field of development finance and the setting of its regulatory frameworks, but also in research, training and publishing, critics express concern about their status as the perceived 'experts' in the area, and the resultant subordination or elimination of alternative discourses that challenge the neoliberal view of development that they expound.

International trade regulation

In addition to setting the framework for the establishment of the IMF and World Bank, the initial Bretton Woods agreement incorporated a plan for the creation of an International Trade Organization (ITO). While these plans were not fulfilled until 1995 with the setting up of the WTO, the Bretton Woods conference laid the ground for a series of meetings on trade regulation under the auspices of the United Nations. These meetings led to the establishment of the General Agreement on Tariffs and Trade (GATT) that, from 1948 until 1994, constituted the rules for a substantial amount of world trade during a period of unprecedented growth in international trade. Despite its development across various rounds of negotiation, GATT was never formalized as a set of binding conditions to which all countries signed up. During periods of economic turmoil in the 1970s and 1980s, accompanied by a resurgence of protectionist policies by national governments, it became apparent that the outcomes of the GATT negotiations were not effective in addressing the complexities of contemporary international trade relations. In 1993, the GATT was revised and further obligations were placed upon signatories. However, the most significant development in this round of negotiations was the agreement that led to the setting up of the World Trade Organization. The WTO was established at the outset as an institutional body that brought together the existing 75 GATT members and those of the European Community.

The World Trade Organization

The main functions of the Geneva-based WTO, that by November 2015 had grown to 162 member countries, include administering trade agreements, constituting a forum for trade negotiations between member countries, handling trade disputes, monitoring national trade policies, providing technical assistance and training for developing countries, and engaging in cooperation with other international organizations. While the main objective of the WTO is the liberalization of world trade, it also declares that its activities can result in a range of positive socio-economic outcomes, including: stimulating economic growth and employment, reducing living costs, improving living standards, enhancing protection of the environment, contributing to world peace and encouraging good governance, while reducing the costs of international business activities. The system of multilateral agreements within the WTO covers trade in goods, services and intellectual property rights.

The key principles set out by the WTO stipulate that member countries should engage in trade with each other without discrimination and should not give preferential treatment to their domestic products and services. These principles are encapsulated within the concept of 'most favoured nation' (MFN). This term used to mean that nations could treat certain countries more favourably than others. Now, however, it indicates that WTO members will grant all members – with a few defined exceptions, including national security, bio-security and fellow members of regional trading blocs – 'most favoured' status. The MFN principle implies that imported goods from other member states, along with services provided and copyrights and patents held by their organizations, will be subject to the same treatment as domestic products, services and intellectual properties. WTO members are obliged to engage in negotiation to remove barriers to trade, and to commit to and be bound by the outcomes of these negotiations. Furthermore, WTO principles discourage practices that are seen as being 'unfair', such as the provision of export subsidies and the 'dumping' of products at below-cost. In the 20 years until 2013, global trade volume almost quadrupled, while WTO members' average tariffs reduced by 15% (WTO, 2015).

Within the terms of general WTO membership, some exceptions to the rules are allowed. First, countries are permitted to establish free trade agreements that apply only to goods traded within WTO member states, thus discriminating against goods from non-members. Second, where one country considers that another is trading its goods unfairly, it can raise barriers against products from that country. Moreover, notwithstanding the key tenet of equality of treatment, the WTO does hold to a principle that confers beneficial status to LDCs, in allowing them additional time, flexibility and preferential terms for adjustment to WTO accession. In addition, developed countries can provide special access to their markets to LDCs, in relation to both goods and services. Finally, LDCs are granted special treatment including exemption from WTO provisions and are allowed to offer government subsidies under certain conditions.

Critiques of the WTO

As outlined above, the WTO concentrates its efforts on the liberalization of trade, according to the belief that free trade is good for all countries, including the poorest ones, as it is supposed to lead to their development. However, critics see problems with the WTO's ideological stance. They point to empirical evidence that shows that free trade does not necessarily lead to development and economic growth. In particular, they argue that trade liberalization has not benefited developing countries. This is because, as developed world governments and transnational firms prove adept at manipulating and applying WTO rules for their own benefit, they deprive developing countries of export opportunities that far exceed the value of the total aid funding provided to them. For example, the 2013 global trade deal signed by WTO member countries' ministers in Bali, with the declared intention of reducing barriers to trade and making customs procedures simpler and more transparent, was criticized by anti-poverty groups. They argued that the deal offered 'a boost for big business at the expense of developing nations', demonstrating that 'the WTO can never be a forum for creating a just and equal global economic system' (Inman, 2013).

Over a period of 14 years from 2001, WTO members pursued the Doha Development Round of trade term negotiations. These were supposed to free up trade in agriculture, services and manufactured goods, and the word 'development' was specifically included to indicate intended benefits for poorer nations. However, at a meeting in Nairobi in December 2015, the Doha Round was finally terminated with no conclusion to the negotiations. Following this meeting, while the WTO proclaimed an '"historic" … package for Africa and the world', critics pointed to the organization's ongoing failure to address issues of economic inequality and continuing poverty. They noted that Africa still accounted for less than 2% of world trade. At the same time, there was a $93bn gap in infrastructure finance, leaving African farmers unable to exploit any market opportunities. Additionally, it was highlighted that $6bn subsidy to US cotton farmers in 2014 undermined prices and markets for West African producers (Watkins, 2015). As the Doha round was put to rest, the USA was heading a drive towards bilateral, regional and sector-specific trade agreements. Critics saw these as a further shift of power to MNCs, including provisions to override nation state legislation, an issue we discuss in the next section.

Academics in the field of environmental studies problematize the key underlying assumption that economic development is good for all nations, and that it should be prioritized over other policy objectives. They point to how the drive to economic growth is dependent upon material improvement through increased gross domestic product (GDP), and that this requires increasing exploitation of finite natural resources. The resultant resource depletion leads to losses of natural habitats and species, and to increasing levels of environmental pollution and global warming. Similarly, human rights groups and trade union movements argue that the WTO does not take sufficient cognizance of issues of child labour, forced labour and other forms of exploitation. In this context, the WTO is criticized for not engaging with social and environmental issues in a meaningful way.

Proponents of the WTO point to the fact that, unlike other transnational agencies such as the International Labour Organization (ILO), it has the power to impose sanctions on member states that transgress its rules. On the other hand, critics highlight that these powers can be fairly limited. Additionally, since the WTO does not issue any loans or provide funding for projects, it cannot apply any punitive financial sanctions through withholding monies. It has also been highlighted that rules of 'equality' of trade are applied in a global marketplace that is already shaped by the inequalities of the past. Here, the new rules of the game do not provide a level playing field. Rather, they prevent developing nations from benefiting their nascent industries by application of the very protectionist policies that enabled the developed countries to achieve their current global dominance.

Economic integration

In addition to those agencies, such as the IMF, World Bank and WTO, that are designed to operate globally at a supranational level, the period after the Second World War saw steady development of a range of regional trade agreements and other forms of localized economic integration in different parts of the world. Many of these were not established for purely economic reasons, such as the removal of trade barriers between members, but to serve also as loci of regional and geopolitical power. A variety of forms and degrees of economic integration exist, as conceptualized by Balassa (1962). These include: the free trade area (FTA), customs union, common market, economic union and political union.

The first category refers to a situation where member countries agree to remove barriers to trade within their trading bloc, yet maintain separate trade policies in relation to non-member states. One example of an FTA is the North American Free Trade-Agreement (NAFTA) that comprises Canada, Mexico and the United States. At the start of 2017, discussions were at an advanced stage to establish two major agreements between the US and other countries: the Trans-Pacific Partnership Agreement (TPP) and the Transatlantic Trade and Investment Partnership (TTIP). The content of these defined rules for market access, regulatory frameworks, and principles for co-operation. However, President Trump withdrew from the TPP soon after taking office. In the case of a customs union, members not only adopt a free trade policy amongst themselves, but they also agree a common trade policy framework for their individual dealings with other countries. At present, we identify no remaining grouping that falls into this category, but in the nineteenth century various principalities that now comprise modern Germany set up such a union, the *Zollverein*.

A common market assumes not only a customs union, but also a free movement of goods, labour and capital within its borders. Both workers and firms are free to relocate, in theory at least, in order to exploit the most advantageous conditions within particular member states. A contemporary example of the common market is MERCOSUR, the grouping of Argentina, Brazil, Paraguay, Uruguay and Venezuela. The fourth step in economic integration is economic union, whereby, in addition to the conditions of a common market, all economic policies, including monetary, fiscal and welfare policies, are set collectively by members. The European Union is the closest empirical example of economic union with, until recently, gradual development towards economic and political integration. At the time of writing, the EU consists of 28 members and constitutes a single market that embraces a number of common policies on trade, agriculture and fisheries, and regional development. Nineteen of the member states have thus far adopted the single European currency, the euro. In addition, the EU incorporates a number of bodies, including the European Commission, the Council of the European Union, the European Council, the European Central Bank, the Court of Justice of the European Union, and the European Parliament. Despite this high level of integration, to date, EU countries still pursue largely individual foreign policies and administer separate internal judicial and security policies. Moreover, following the UK referendum decision to exit the EU – so-called 'Brexit' – the European Union faces a reduction in the number of its members for the first time in its history, and reduced integration.

Political union itself represents total integration of two or more countries into one, whereby each vests political and economic sovereignty in the new nation and relinquishes all national institutions. The reunification of East and West Germany in 1990 provides an example of the establishment of such a political union.

Critiques of economic integration

Extant examples of economic blocs and other types of integration show various forms of regionalization, whereby economic cooperation and interdependence increase within specific geographic areas. Proponents of this trend point to its positive outcomes for the involved countries in terms of expansion of markets and overall economic growth. Critics, however, emphasize how the benefits of economic integration are often not distributed equally amongst all parties. For example, in the case of NAFTA, it is pointed out that American firms are able to set up operations in Mexico in order to exploit a pool of cheap labour and less constraining operating conditions. At the same time, however, the USA maintains and currently aims to reinforce controls on immigration by Mexicans who seek to take advantage of employment and business opportunities in the United States. As Mexican markets have opened up for American companies, so the Mexican economy has become more and more dependent upon and tied to that of its powerful neighbour. This, some argue, has led to a reduction in Mexico's chances of competing effectively in the international economic arena on its own terms. They highlight that much of the country's export earnings, along with employment opportunities for its workforce, is tied to production by US (plus Japanese and EU) firms located in the *maquiladoras*, the export processing zones (EPZs) that enable them to operate largely outside Mexican taxation and import/export duty frameworks.

The espoused and actual benefits of membership of the European Union have also been contested. While it is acknowledged that the EU has provided a platform for greater political and social stability in post-Second World War Europe, some point out that, in its current form, it does not offer equal advantages for all its members. The Union was built on principles of free movement of goods, services, capital and people and the realization of these was the case for early entrants. However, these were not initially granted to the accession countries which joined in 2004 and 2006, as selective limits were applied, for example, on the movement of workers. More recently, mass migration into Europe from Africa and the Middle East, along with the result of the 'Brexit' referendum, have surfaced political and social tensions associated with and manifested through calls for limiting freedom of movement of individuals within the EU.

One of the Union's ideals was that member countries would support each other's development and provide help in crisis situations. Countries such as Greece and Ireland used to be held up as examples of economies whose development greatly benefited from EU membership. However, following the GFC, both countries fell into rapid decline that in the case of Greece culminated in the default on debt repayments. As outlined previously, some blamed other EU governments for refusing debt relief since this would have exposed their own banks to potential collapse as holders of these debts, and as such, for not living up to the Union's ideals of mutual support.

Even before President Trump withdrew from the TPP, both this and the TIPP agreement evoked substantial controversy. The TPP was to be a plurilateral agreement involving 12 nations: Australia, Brunei Darussalam, Canada, Chile, Japan, Malaysia, Mexico, New Zealand, Peru, Singapore, the US and Vietnam, together representing around 40% of global GDP. While the negotiators acclaimed the agreement as providing significant outcomes in removing barriers to trade in goods and services, and investment between the signatories, critics expressed a range of concerns about it and its potential negative consequences for governments and societies, consumers, workers and the environment. For example, the economist Robert Reich (2015) described it as a 'Trojan horse in a global race to the bottom, giving big corporations and Wall Street banks a way to eliminate any and all laws and regulations that get in the way of their profits'. Following release of the full text of the agreement, Andrew Robb, Australian trade minister speaking on environmental policy, praised it as one that 'does provide safeguards, the best safeguards that have ever been provided in any agreement' (Hill, 2015). However, George Kahale III, chairman of the world's leading arbitration firm, countered by stating 'If the trade minister is saying "we're not at risk of regulating for environmental matters", then the trade minister is wrong' (ibid.). Kahale also commented critically on Robb's statements that Australians need not worry about the TPP and the implementation of new Investor–State Dispute Settlement (ISDS) provisions. He confirmed that the TPP makes provisions for foreign corporations to use ISDS to make claims against the Australian government if their profits are affected by any Australian law and policy. This, of course, would apply across all members. In general, there are serious concerns that the deal, that has been negotiated behind closed doors, privileges the interests of MNCs over those of governments and societies, and is underpinned by a view of people as consumers rather than citizens.

Similar debates surround the TIPP, a proposed bilateral agreement between the European Union and the USA, also negotiated in secrecy. The agreement has given rise to protests by charities, environmentalists, NGOs and trade unions, and has been described by the executive director of the campaign organization War on Want as 'An assault on European and US societies by transnational corporation' (Williams, 2015).

Overall, while some see regional economic integration as providing benefits in expanding markets and opportunities, others consider it as reinforcing economic and political domination by both the already powerful nations within any given bloc and by big business. Moreover, critics point out that this integration takes place largely around the imperative of economic growth and, thereby, other objectives, including those of a social and environmental nature, are subjugated to this end.

Conclusion

In this chapter, we presented an overview of the institutional frameworks of contemporary IB, outlining the role of the Bretton Woods conference in establishing the current transnational economic institutions. We started by explaining the origins and development of the international monetary system, and pointed to its roots in British imperialism. We discussed the main principles of the Bretton Woods system of exchange rates and the reasons behind its failure. In addition, we offered some recent examples of the mechanisms by which currency exchange rates are determined.

Following our discussion of the international monetary system, we introduced the major transnational institutions underpinning global economic activity, namely, the IMF, the World Bank and the WTO. Having provided background information about their aims and activities, we presented some of the criticisms that, over time, have been directed at them. We highlighted how the principles of the IMF, the World Bank and the WTO are grounded in the doctrine of neoliberalism and we commented on how, outside the discourse of neoliberal thinking, these have been criticized and challenged. Most notably, we introduced discussion about the impact of these three institutions upon the economic situation of developing countries.

We also considered different forms and institutions of economic integration. We explained the principles behind, and gave examples of, the main forms of such integration, including the free trade area, customs union, common market, economic union and political union. We also discussed some critiques of economic integration. Having considered how regional economic blocs contribute to maintaining and reinforcing unequal power relations between nation states within the international political economy, we drew particular attention to contemporary debate and controversy over two major regional trade agreement proposals, the TTP and TTIP.

Questions

1. In what ways have the Bretton Woods institutions shaped the conditions of IB development since the Second World War, and how is their influence evident in the present?
2. How does formal economic integration in different parts of the world reflect the current distribution of power amongst participating nation states?
3. Since the publication of this text, what developments have taken place in relation to the TTP and TTIP, and which stakeholders have been the most powerful ones in bringing these about?

Further reading

Bretton Woods Project (2016) *Topics*. Available at: www.brettonwoods project.org/ (accessed 22 September 2016).

McDonagh, L. (2015) 'How the secret TTIP trade deal could enable companies to sue countries', *The Conversation*, 12 November. Available at: http://theconversation.com/how-the-secret-ttip-trade-deal-could-enable-companies-to-sue-countries-50543 (accessed 22 September 2016).

Smith, H. (2016) 'A year after the crisis was declared over, Greece is still spiralling down', *The Economist*, 14 August. Available at: www.theguardian.com/business/2016/aug/13/greek-economy-still-spiralling-down-year-after-crisis-declared-over (accessed 22 September 2016).

4

The International Business Organization

Introduction

So far, in this book, we have discussed the origins of international business, theories of IB and the supranational agencies that provide the institutional context of IB. Notwithstanding its early grounding in trade between countries, contemporary understanding of IB for many will be linked to thinking on the multinational corporation, on global brands such as HSBC, McDonald's and Samsung, on banking failures in the wake of the GFC such as the Lehmann Brothers collapse, and on major events of environmental damage such as BP's Deepwater Horizon oil spill. In this chapter, we discuss the origins and development of MNCs and, in particular, how they have been and remain more than just organizations of commerce, that can be seen as benign in the fields of business, politics, society and environment, and frequently have close links to the political agendas of their home countries. We look at both historical and more recent examples of the international firm in order to explain its significance.

Colonial expansion and the internationalization of business

As pointed out at the beginning of this book, international trade as an activity has existed for millennia. The emergence of the international firm, however, can be traced to European colonial expansion in the era of geographical exploration. The historical importance of the connection between political interests of the nation state and internationalization of commercial organizations can be illustrated through the examples of the Honourable East India Company (HEIC) and the Dutch East India Company (Vereenigde Oostindische Compagnie, or VOC). These privately owned commercial organizations were key drivers of and actors in English and Dutch colonial expansion, respectively, and in the spread of capitalism. The HEIC, with 125 merchant shareholders, was granted a Royal Charter on 31 December 1600, and for over 250 years in various forms it grew and developed to the stage where its officials practically ruled the sub-continent on behalf of the British government. The company initially established trading rights with Emperor Jahangir, ruler of the Mughal Empire. This gave the HEIC exclusive rights to develop bases and to acquire local goods and resources, such as tea, silk and dyes, in return for providing European luxury goods to the emperors and their courts.

Over its history, the company maintained a relationship with Parliament that saw its powers ebb and flow. At various times it held rights to mint currency, acquire territories, establish its own military forces, exercise legal powers, and make war and peace on behalf of the country. By the mid-eighteenth century, the Mughal Empire had disintegrated, to be replaced by a number of regional states. While this was not a period of instability, members of the HEIC were able to exploit the fragmentation and assert their power and influence. Competing British and French colonialists initially allied themselves with different local factions to seek to maximize their territorial advantage. The British forces, led by Robert Clive, succeeded in taking control of Bengal. As the British asserted their power, company governors became state governors, with company governor-general Richard, later Marquess, Wellesley using military power to impose hegemonic British rule over an area that latterly extended from modern-day Burma/Myanmar in the south-east to Afghanistan in the north-west. After the first 100 years of its existence, the company had become more an agent of government than a trading company, and following the loss of its trade monopoly in 1813 it ceased all trading activities. After running up mounting losses on its administrative and military functions, it was finally nationalized and dissolved in 1874. However, its administrative legacy laid the basis for the development of the British Civil Service.

During the period in which the HEIC established English, then British, colonialism in India, the VOC similarly played a leading role in Dutch colonization of South East Asia. Whilst the HEIC was a wholly British venture, the VOC was the world's first multinational enterprise, with shareholders from Germany and what are now Belgium and Luxembourg. By the end of the seventeenth century, with establishments in areas that include modern Bangladesh, Iran, Malaysia, Taiwan, Thailand and southern China, the company not only had a substantial establishment of merchant ships and employees, but also a fleet of 40 warships and an army of 10,000 soldiers. In 1641, following the expulsion of Portuguese traders by the Japanese, the VOC established a trading post on the artificial island of Dejima in Nagasaki Bay. From 1641 until 1853, this was the only means by which Europeans could trade with Japan. In addition to its peaceful trading activities, however, the company was implicated in the use of forced repatriation and the killing of native populations as a tool of business development in the Banda Islands, part of modern Indonesia.

These two examples illustrate how geographical expansion of nation states in pursuit of their colonialist and imperialist ambitions was interlinked with the growth of companies and the spread of capitalist enterprise across the world. The establishment of the conditions for these companies to trade in and from the new territories was made possible through the use of military power, sometimes without the explicit sanction of the home country government. In the rest of this chapter we look not only at the growth and expansion of the contemporary MNC and its social, economic and environmental impacts, but also at the present-day linkage of some MNCs to the government of their country of origin, and to the application of military force in their countries of operation.

Technological development and the internationalization of business

Discussing the emergence of IB from an historical perspective, as well as in the political context, the development of technology has been of primary importance in creating conditions for nation states to colonize overseas territories, and for capitalist organizations to extend their operations internationally. Steger (2013) explains how the expansionist aspirations of European powers were assisted by the invention of mechanized printing, developments in wind and water mill technologies, advancements in navigation techniques and sea transportation, and the development of extensive postal systems.

Over time, the ability to transport goods and people facilitated the internationalization of business, as railways, mechanized shipping and, more recently, intercontinental air transport were developed. Furthermore, the invention of the telegraph and, later, the telephone and radio provided vastly increased speed of communication across the world. This allowed both governments and businesses to control their activities from a central point more effectively. By 1866 Europe and North America were connected by undersea telegraph cable, while by 1890 all the major colonies of the British Empire were cabled from the UK. Subsequently, undersea telegraph cables were replaced by telephone cables and, in parallel, radio communication was developed. Now, of course, we have the Internet and satellite-based global communications networks.

Technological advancement has enabled the emergence of new ways of doing business, new business models in existing fields, and wholly new types of business. Examples of these three developments include, respectively: Internet banking; fast fashion clothes retailing; and social media platforms. In recent decades, there have been major advances in the fields of information technology (IT) and telecommunications – often referred to jointly as information and communications technologies (ICTs). New ICTs, however, are not the only, or the major, technological enablers of internationalization. Before we address their contribution, we discuss how incremental development of earlier technologies has had a major impact on the growth of IB.

In the field of shipping, since the Second World War new forms of mass sea transportation have been introduced, permitting organizations to engage in global transfer of a wide range of raw materials and finished products. The development of containerization has allowed the growth of international logistics networks for moving large amounts of goods at relatively low cost in small units. Modularized containers are carried not just on ships, through a global network of major ports like Rotterdam, New Orleans, Shanghai and Singapore, but also by rail and road – in a single unit from their source to their final destination. In addition, the major petroleum refining companies now distribute oil products globally in 'very large crude carriers' (VLCCs), while automobile companies move cars, trucks and other vehicles around the world on huge 'roll-on, roll-off' (Ro-Ro) vessels.

There have been major advancements in air transportation during the same period but, while these offer speed of global goods movement, air remains considerably more expensive than sea transportation. Therefore, it is used by companies primarily for the purpose of moving people or those products that need to be transported rapidly and in relatively small and high value packages. These developments in logistics and transportation technology have facilitated the growth of international business and, as such, benefited companies. However, they have not had an equally positive effect on all stakeholders within IB, in particular through their detrimental impact upon the natural environment. Air transportation has been subject to criticism for its level of carbon emissions, in large part due to the growth in low-cost airlines across the world. A report from the Global Commission on Economy and Climate (Gençsü and Hino, 2015) indicates that shipping is responsible for 3% of global CO_2 emissions, and aviation for 2%. These emissions continue to increase and it is estimated that by 2050 they will reach a combined total of between 10% and 32% of global carbon dioxide emissions.

The issue of global warming and climate change is generally recognized as linked to the level of emissions. In this context, serious questions need to be asked as to whether we should celebrate the opportunities for global market and supply chain expansion by IB or, rather, be concerned about the impact of the resultant environmental damage upon the future of planet Earth. In our view, the environmental effects arising from the internationalization of businesses, especially those operating at a global level, create an urgent need for thinking about what kind of, and to what extent, IB practices should be encouraged and considered as positive.

The contribution of new ICTs in the last few decades has grown exponentially, as the power and speed of technologies has multiplied. The development of the Internet, spread of mobile communications, the emergence of social media platforms and the overall rise of the digital economy have enabled individuals and businesses to communicate instantaneously from any location and to pass vast amounts of data and information securely. The ability to complete transactions without spatiotemporal constraints has, in turn, contributed to the financialization of the contemporary economy. New ICTs have not only supported new ways for businesses and their people to organize globally, but they have also provided the means for emerging counterforces to organize and rally support against governments and businesses, and their activities, as we discuss in Chapter 5.

The technologically-facilitated increase in international financial flows coupled with financial liberalization, has made it possible for companies and individuals in one country to purchase shares, finance property development or borrow and locate funds in banks abroad to a much greater extent than in the past. While the growth of international finance constitutes a significant aspect of the development of IB activities in recent times, it has also brought about a stronger drive for shareholder value and a higher frequency of financial crises, affecting economies of both rich and developing countries. In the context of the GFC, the same digital technologies that have enabled high-speed flow of information within global financial markets, have been blamed for contributing to the crisis through creating and sustaining 'the reckless and myopic culture of risk and unhinged speculation' (Chakravartty and Downing, 2010: 693) associated with these markets.

We have provided an overview of the historical antecedents of the contemporary MNC along with the political, economic and technological factors that have underpinned and supported its growth. We have also offered a critical commentary on key aspects of these. Below, we consider the ways in which firms go about internationalizing.

Internationalization of companies

As Porter (1985) argues, firms may adopt a number of strategies in seeking to gain 'competitive advantage' through internationalizing. A central theme of contemporary internationalization is the drive to configure the company 'value chain' (Porter, 1985) to increase efficiency, make most effective use of resources and to maximize profits. Traditionally, as explained in Chapter 2, internationalization of the firm has been seen to proceed according to the model of gradual involvement in international activities. This model suggests that companies wishing to internationalize normally start from employing market entry strategies that require a low level of engagement in operations abroad, before moving on to more advanced forms of IB presence. It is usually assumed that firms will decide to grow internationally for a number of reasons. These might include an anticipated increase in profitability, or an expectation of delivering a product or service that is not currently available in a foreign market. Alternatively, firms may desire to take advantage of expertise they might have about a foreign market, to benefit from tax subsidies available abroad or to generate economies of scale through increasing production to meet international demand. Moreover, companies may choose to start operating abroad in order to respond to competitive pressures, to counter the decline in demand within the domestic market, or to utilize excess production capacity. They may also wish to seize the opportunity to expand through serving a foreign market located within a close geographic or psychological distance from the domestic one, and that can be entered relatively easily. In the case of previously mentioned 'born globals', companies might operate internationally from the outset, rather than by incremental internationalization. Firms may choose between a range of 'modes of market entry', such as exporting and importing, licensing, franchising, short- and long-term alliances, subcontracting, and merger and acquisition. In the space of this book, we cannot discuss all of these in depth, and would refer you to texts that discuss these in more detail.

As with many other IB theories and concepts, market entry modes are considered from the perspective of the firm as the central actor whose potential advantages and risks are assessed. However, the selected strategies of internationalization also have impacts upon other stakeholders in IB. As previously discussed, global logistics and transportation will, in the case of each of the market entry modes, affect the natural environment and the society. In configuring their value chains internationally and globally through sub-contracting, firms are able to take advantage of geographical locations of production with the lowest cost structures. Those who work for sub-contractor companies of MNCs (e.g. the producers of the majority of consumer goods) are often based in developing countries and are employed at a low wage and under precarious working conditions. Since they are not the direct employees of the MNC but of the sub-contractor, the multinational company that benefits from their labour does not have the legal responsibility for ensuring that the labour practices of the sub-contractor are the same as those that the MNC would have to obey in its home country. We return to this issue in Chapter 6.

Another example of possible negative impacts of a market entry strategy upon a party other than the shareholders of the companies involved can be found in the case of mergers and acquisitions. This strategy of internationalization can benefit firms not only through providing them with access to new markets, resources and expertise, but can potentially lead to lowering costs through reducing the number of employees. Where this happens, the post-merger or post-acquisition company may have lower staff costs than the two entities prior to the merger or acquisition. This will mean the loss of jobs for a number of people and of the source of income for them and their families. This may then require government to provide the individuals affected with unemployment benefits, if these are offered in the particular country. It needs to be borne in mind, however, that such benefits are not generally available to the unemployed in developing economies. Merger and acquisition activity at an international level can also contribute to an increase in the market power of companies pursuing this strategy. As a consequence of this, the firm may gain a higher degree of influence upon the price levels in its industry. This, is turn, may disadvantage the customers, who will have to pay a higher price for the products than they would if prices were determined under more competitive conditions.

From the outline of the various strategies of internationalization, it would be possible to infer that through a process of gradual expansion, MNCs grow into geographically evenly spread entities, with a similar type of presence across the world. However, despite the globalization of economic activity, control over the world's MNCs is executed from relatively few locations. The top 20 companies by revenue generation in the *Fortune 500* global list for 2015 includes eight firms with head-quarters in Europe, six based in the US, four from China, and one each from Japan and South Korea (Fortune, 2016). These examples lead us to a consideration of the economic and political power of MNCs in the contemporary world.

Economic and political power of multinational corporations

When asked to give the names of well-known MNCs, most people will immediately think in terms of global consumer brands, such as Apple, BMW, Google or Samsung. Few are aware of the scale of contemporary MNCs' economic power, and of the fact that their revenues frequently exceed the GDP of entire countries. For example, Walmart and Sinopec, with revenues of $486 billion and $447 billion, respectively, in 2014 would lie at numbers 27 and 28 in the list of countries, between Norway and Austria (United Nations, 2015). Meanwhile, the revenues of Royal Dutch Shell and China National Petroleum in 2014 would place at numbers 28 and 29, between Austria and Iran, while Exxon Mobil would lie at 31, between United Arab Emirates and Venezuela.

The list of the largest commercial players in contemporary IB is dominated by petroleum refiners. Of the *Fortune 500*, the five companies that followed Walmart in terms of 2014 revenue all operated in this field, namely: Sinopec, Royal Dutch Shell, China National Petroleum, Exxon Mobil and BP. Almost a decade earlier, two Chinese companies, both oil refining, appeared in the list of the top 25 revenue earners. In 2014, there were four. Meanwhile, the Industrial and Commercial Bank of China had grown to become the company with the highest profits in the world – nearly $45bn. To illustrate the enormity of these profits, they were slightly greater than the entire GDP of Serbia, twice as high as the GDP of Cyprus, and around four times that of Macedonia.

The scale and spread of their resources gives these organizations vast amounts of power and influence within the spheres of both economics and politics. While some critics see in the growing power of MNCs a decline in the relevance of the nation state, others point to the way in which neoliberal governments and large capitalist organizations support each other's interests. Businesses sponsor political parties and electoral campaigns at a national level to ensure that, through lobbyists, they will influence policymaking to their own advantage. For instance, in the context of American politics, in the period between 2002 and 2014, major US-based MNCs like Boeing, Exxon Mobil, General Electric, Microsoft, Pfizer and Time Warner provided multimillion dollar donations to support campaigns. Some, such as General Electric and Microsoft gave almost equal contributions to both Democrat and Republican parties. In contrast, others, for example Exxon Mobil and Time Warner, showed clear preference to one or other party. Similar large donations were made by banks, including Goldman Sachs, Bank of America and Citigroup (Open Secrets, 2016a).

The influence of business over policymaking by national governments is seen as an important issue by Transparency International. In a 2015 report the organization raised concerns about the politics–business nexus at the European level. The report drew attention to the ability of large corporations with ample resources to undertake their own lobbying activities, without the need to rely on business associations. This is coupled with widespread practice of 'revolving doors' in all European countries, whereby former government officials become appointed to high positions in businesses. This potentially leads to 'abuse of power and misuse of office or former office' (Transparency International, 2015a: 17). In the UK context, Cave and Rowell (2014) have expressed concerns about the number of senior officials, in particular from the Department of Health and the Ministry of Defence, who left the public sector to take up senior positions in private sector organizations. In 2011–2012 alone, 231 military officers moved to posts in arms- and defence-related companies, a sector in which the UK comes second in the world in terms of international sales. The authors point out that the government was the industry's biggest customer, and the Ministry's close relations with its suppliers were widely recognized. This closeness was discussed in relation to 'disastrously expensive contracts that deliver poor value for taxpayers and often poor performance for the military' (Cave and Rowell, 2014).

In addition to their involvements in political lobbying, MNCs have a record – some might say questionable – of funding scientific research that supports their vested interests. The tobacco industry has a history of sponsoring research that seeks to show that the generally recognized health risks of smoking are over-rated or non-existent (Brownell and Warner, 2009). Similarly, ExxonMobil is reported (Goldenberg, 2015) to be a major funder of groups that are labelled 'climate change sceptics'. Overall, the effects of the activities of MNCs go far beyond their bottom line. Through their broader economic and political impacts, large capitalist organizations influence everybody in society to an extent that many may not realize. To illustrate this point, in the following section we consider a variety of social impacts of Walmart, the world's largest private company, in terms of both revenues and number of employees.

Rhetoric and reality of Walmart

The example of Walmart is worthy of consideration because of the insights it offers into the relationship between the organization of business activities by MNCs and the direction of change within contemporary society. Founded in the small American town of Bentonville, Arkansas in 1962 by Sam Walton, by 2015 the retail chain Walmart had more than 4,500 retail outlets located in 27 countries and serving nearly 260 million customers weekly. In these, products from around the globe were sold by over 2.2 million workers – referred to as 'associates' – with 800,000 employed in countries outside the USA (Walmart, 2015a).

Walmart (2015a) presents itself in a positive light in relation to its economic, social and environmental credentials. The company emphasizes that it treats its responsibilities towards stakeholders seriously, working closely with its suppliers, creating opportunities for its associates worldwide, and providing savings for consumers. It expresses an aspiration to contribute not only to its own growth, but also 'to global responsibility initiatives that make our world better' (Walmart, 2015a: 3). In setting out its commitment to people, the company articulates a belief that 'engaged associates fuel [its] success'. It encourages individuals to join the firm by promising new recruits that 'regardless of your background, Walmart will give you the opportunity to grow a career as far as your ability and hard work will take you' (Walmart, 2015a: 3). Walmart's President and CEO, Doug McMillon, is held up as a prime example of an individual who has benefited from the meritocratic system of advancement through Walmart's ranks, starting his career 'as an hourly associate' and growing 'into roles with increased responsibility' (Walmart, 2015a: 3).

In relation to stakeholder engagement, Walmart (2015b) outlines its priorities in three areas: increasing economic opportunity (including associate opportunity, supplier/small business development, women's economic empowerment and retail sector workforce mobility); sustainability (including leading in energy, zero waste, sustainable food, sustainable materials and manufacturing); and strengthening local communities (including community development, associate philanthropy and support, and disaster response and preparedness). Working towards the achievement of each of these is expected to generate both positive business and societal impacts. Among the former, Walmart lists greater productivity and sales, lower costs, increased supply security and higher associate engagement. The latter include: frontline workforce mobility; creation of new jobs and livelihoods; increased worker safety; reduced greenhouse gas emissions and increased natural capital; greater social cohesion; and disaster mitigation (Walmart, 2015b).

Walmart's bright image of itself is not, however, shared by all. Egan (2014) refers to the company as 'a big part of the problem' of income inequality in the USA. Putting into question Walmart's contribution to the communities where it sets up operations, he contends that 'with its poverty wage structure ... Walmart is a net drain on taxpayers'. A 2014 report by Americans for Tax Fairness illustrates the problematic nature of the company's impact on American society. The report shows that Walmart's enormous profits make the six Walton heirs the richest family in the USA, with a total wealth equal to that of 49 million American families combined (Americans for Tax Fairness, 2014). At the same time, it is estimated that Walmart benefits from over \$7.8 billion per year in American government subsidies of different kinds. The majority of these funds, around \$6.2 billion, come from federal subsidies. These take the form of payment for healthcare, food stamps, and other public assistance programmes designed to help low income earners, such as the National School Lunch Program, School Breakfast Program, Section 8 Housing Program, Earned Income Tax Credit, and Low Income Home Energy Assistance Program. These subsidies constitute a form of taxpayers' 'compensation' for the low wages Walmart pays its associates, who on average earn around \$15,500 annually when working full-time. The extreme inequality between the wealth of the company's owners and its workers has been recognized as an issue by American politicians. During the 2016 presidential campaign, the Democratic contender Bernie Sanders referred to it as 'unacceptable that the Waltons have more wealth than the bottom 40% of Americans' and that 'the Walton family refuses to pay their workers a living wage' (Neate, 2016).

In addition to being criticized for its low wages regime, over the years Walmart has gained a reputation for worker discrimination on the basis of gender and race, for suppressing workers' rights, and for failing to ensure worker safety. In 2012, almost 2,000 Walmart women workers filed charges against the company for alleged gender discrimination with regard to pay and promotion (Hines, 2012). The company's practices of unlawful disciplinary actions against its associates have also resulted in a number of charges brought to the National Labor Relations Board. In relation to work safety conditions, independent inspections carried out in factories producing goods for Walmart in Bangladesh in 2013 revealed that 32 out of 200 factories 'required urgent work to fix serious failings, including one factory that was so unsafe it had to be shut down and another with an illegal eighth floor containing the staff canteen' (Butler, 2013). The inspections took place following the collapse of the Rana Plaza building, in which more than 1,100 garment workers died.

Environmental groups have expressed concerns about Walmart's climate change record. According to a 2013 report by the Institute for Local Self-Reliance, a non-profit research and educational organization in the USA, the company's 'greenhouse gas emissions have grown substantially and are continuing to rise' and Walmart 'lags its peers in making the shift to renewable power' (ILSR, 2013: 4). The report also explains that the company fails to report on the full extent of its pollution impact, for example through omitting from its environmental reporting the effects on the environment of its global shipping operations and land development practices. The report also draws attention to Walmart's contributions to the political campaigns of those 'politicians who oppose action on the climate crisis, helping to ensure that the U.S. does not take the steps necessary to avert the worst impacts of global warming' (ILSR, 2013: 4).

Organization and militarization

The contemporary world of IB demonstrates features that we have highlighted in history and that are not often discussed in mainstream literature. Earlier, we discussed how the common interests of governments and private capital in pursuit of geographic expansion were often supported by private armies. We can identify MNCs now that operate as the HEIC and VOC did in the past to promote home government agendas in other countries. In post-invasion Iraq, American corporations provided logistical and maintenance support for the armed forces and for other companies. However, several engaged in activities that would normally be considered the responsibility of the formal military, including carrying weapons to enforce security. While this paramilitary activity generally forms a small part of the MNC's overall activities, the effects can be devastating and long lasting. For example, the conviction in their home country of four former members of the US Blackwater corporation (later reborn as Academi) private security arm for the murder of 14 Iraqi civilians in 2007 created widespread outrage and criticism (BBC, 2014).

In recent years, concerns have been raised by various groups (e.g. Corporate Watch, 2016; Milmo, 2015) about the ties between developed world governments and MNCs in relation to the international sale of weapons, particularly to impoverished nations and/or those with unstable political regimes. UK based MNC, BAE Systems has been the subject of numerous investigations and reports in relation to the sale of military hardware (cf. Durham, 2015). The firm has business operations in the UK, USA, Saudi Arabia, India and Australia. It defines itself and its corporate responsibility strategy as follows: 'Our vision is to be the premier global defence, aerospace and security company. Responsible behaviour is one of four pillars of our Company strategy, together with customer focus, program execution and financial performance' (BAE Systems, 2016). In the 1990s, BAE (then British Aerospace) was subject to a wave of criticism for selling 16 of its Hawk 'multi-role combat aircraft' to Indonesia, with UK government support, at a time when that nation was repressing the population of East Timor through military action, including alleged air attacks on civilian targets by Hawks supplied previously (Monbiot, 1996). Among the leading critics of the deal was then Labour Opposition MP Robin Cook, who as Foreign Secretary in the Labour government of 1997 renewed the export licence (*The Guardian*, 1999). Cook was later to write of the company's access to the very top level of government, that the CEO appeared to have 'the key to the garden door' of the Prime Minister's residence (McSmith, 2009). BAE's international engagement with government is further illustrated by year-on-year spends of millions of dollars on political lobbying in the USA (Open Secrets, 2016b). In 2010, following decades of denial of wrongdoing, the company settled inquiries with both the US Department of Justice and the UK Serious Fraud Office, paying almost £300m in penalties for false accounting in relation to sales of armaments, including to poverty-stricken Tanzania, to which £30m of the penalties were redirected (Leigh and Evans, 2010).

Another MNC that has been subject to critical analysis is American firm Northrop Grumman. One of its subsidiaries, Vinnell Corporation, offers a wide range of military services in the international arena. Some of these provide support for its own home government abroad, such as in fulfilling Department of Defense contracts for operations and maintenance services at US air bases in Saudi Arabia and Oman (Sourcewatch, 2006a). Through its joint venture partnership, Vinnell Arabia, the company has also provided long-term support to the Saudi National Guard (Sourcewatch, 2006b; Vinnell Arabia, 2016). On its own website, the company describes itself as 'the leader in U.S. military doctrine-based training, logistics and support services inside Saudi Arabia' (Vinnell Arabia, 2016). In response to these activities, the company has attracted several terrorist attacks against its facilities and personnel in Saudi Arabia (cf. Sourcewatch, 2006b).

In addition to examples of MNC involvement in providing military hardware and training, the aftermath of the US-led invasions of Afghanistan and Iraq raised many questions about the engagement of private companies in both the lucrative 'rebuilding' programmes and in the provision of 'private security' – what in the past would have been referred to as mercenary armies. In relation to rebuilding in Iraq, American MNCs were awarded billions of US dollars in contracts. Firms like Bechtel and Parsons were regular contributors to both major political parties over decades and employed 'revolving door' personnel – individuals who had previously held senior public sector posts (cf. Open Secrets, 2016c). In the aftermath of these invasions, as the numbers of US military personnel actively engaged declined, there was a transfer of responsibility and control to largely US-based MNCs. However, data indicate that the actual operations were to a major extent undertaken by outsourced contract labour, some from local communities, but many brought in from outside of both the USA and the 'host' country and referred to as 'third country nationals' (TCNs) by the US Pentagon (Li, 2015). Data show that TCNs equalled or outnumbered both US and local numbers in Iraq, with Ugandans undertaking perimeter security operations for US bases in both Iraq and Afghanistan, and with 10,000 reportedly working in Iraq alone at one point (Li, 2015).

While the controversial Blackwater company we refer to above no longer exists in name, its operations continue after several re-brandings. In 2014, the founder, Erik Prince, told an American conservative group meeting that, had the Obama administration not 'crushed' the former Blackwater business, it 'could have successfully combatted militant group Islamic State' (RT.com, 2014). This report also lists how, despite its apparent negative view of the company, the Obama administration had awarded contracts worth over $500m to the reborn Academi brand. This illustrates how, as with BAE Systems, relationships between the military–industrial machine and government live beyond changes of administration and through critical issues and negative reporting.

In the above sections, we discussed examples of connections between major US- and UK-based MNCs and government, and with activities that have been widely criticized and, in some cases, punished through courts and inquiries. However, not all examples of such activities arise from these countries or are as widely reported. The Stockholm International Peace Research Institute (SIPRI, 2016a) recorded that the top five major arms export nations in 2015, in order, were the USA, Russia, Germany, France and China, while the top five importers were Saudi Arabia, India, Australia, Egypt and United Arab Emirates. Meanwhile, the four nations with the largest expenditure on arms in 2015 – the USA, China, Saudi Arabia and Russia – together spent almost $965 billion on weapons systems (SIPRI, 2016b).

Beyond military and paramilitary IB activity, there are other aspects of international trade that are underpinned by military-like force. Links have been identified between MNCs from the USA, Europe and China, and trade in ores used in tin production, industrial diamonds and coltan – an ore that supplies essential minerals for use in advanced electronics systems, ranging from mobile phone to electric car batteries. Mining and extraction in the Democratic Republic of Congo (DRC), the world's richest country in mineral reserves, is reportedly underpinned by violence (cf. Ayres, 2012). The DRC is a country that has been ravaged by internal strife, where the civilian population has been subjected to systematic pillage, rape and torture by soldiers of the private armies of a host of warlords, some supported by the armies of neighbouring countries. This is a population for whom there is no reward from the country's vast wealth (see Amnesty International, 2016).

Conclusion

In this chapter, we looked at the major commercial actor in IB – the MNC – from an historical and a contemporary perspective. We focused on the link between firms operating internationally and the spheres of politics, the economy, society and the environment. By reference to historical examples of the HEIC and VOC, we explained how, over time, the growth of international companies was facilitated by and contributed to the geographical expansion of the European powers and to the development of capitalism as the dominant economic system.

We outlined key developments in technology that influenced the growth of IB. We also drew attention to advances in transportation and logistics, production technologies and communication, and to their role in promoting IB activities through enabling time and cost-efficient transfer of goods, people, information and capital. Following our discussion of the historical influences on the growth of MNCs, we addressed issues relating to the functioning of capitalist organizations in contemporary IB. Having listed the various modes of market entry available to firms, we commented on how some of them impact stakeholders other than the companies' shareholders. We also reflected upon the economic and political power of MNCs. We elaborated on the case of Walmart, as an exemplification of the problematic nature of corporate success, whereby international growth and high financial performance, coupled with low prices for the consumer, have come at a high cost for the workers, the taxpayers and the environment.

Finally, we drew attention to an additional aspect of IB that is absent from most of the mainstream accounts – how MNCs from developed economies benefit from military conflict. Highlighting the past and present interdependencies between companies operating internationally and politics, the economy, society and the environment has allowed us to show that, through their diverse impacts, IB activities are not just relevant to the involved firms and their shareholders, but to everybody in society, both in the present and in the future.

Questions

1. In what ways has shipping containerization influenced the activities of MNCs, and which political and economic factors have enabled these changes to happen?
2. What insights into the power dynamics of the IB environment can be gained by considering that the largest MNCs' revenues exceed the GDP of some nations?
3. What are the moral and ethical implications of MNCs' engagement in militarization – both in arms sales and provision of private armies?

Further reading

Goetz, S.J. and Swaminathan, H. (2006) 'Wal-Mart and country-wide poverty', *Social Science Quarterly*, 87: 211–226. Available at: http://sehn.igc.org/tccpdf/Wal-Mart%20and%20poverty.pdf (accessed 22 September 2016).

Ritholtz, B. (2015) 'Wal-Mart learns to live without everyday poverty wages', *Bloomberg View*, 11 June. Available at: www.bloomberg.com/view/articles/2015-06-11/wal-mart-lives-without-everyday-poverty-wages (accessed 22 September 2016).

Shaver, J.M. (2013) 'Do we really need more entry mode studies?', *Journal of International Business Studies*, 44: 23–27. Available at: www.paceth.com/ibus/jibs201224a.pdf (accessed 22 September 2016).

5

The Dynamic Landscape of International Business

▰▰▰▰ Introduction

To this point, we have looked at how the field of IB developed historically and how we have ended up in the position we find ourselves in now. While much of this trajectory has been gradual and substantive change has been spread over decades and even centuries, we are currently witnessing an age of rapidly accelerating technological change and socio-political and economic disruption. In the past decade, we have seen the emergence of new economic powers at the nation state level along with novel business models that are totally reliant on new Internet technologies. However, we also find challenges to the strength and longevity of some changes, indicating that what were considered long-term trends may be less significant when assessed retrospectively.

Discussing these ideas in terms of the new dynamic landscape of IB, we must consider changes in the relative economic standing of countries and how these are represented and driven by analysts' interpretations. In addition, we need to address the impact of the major event of the twenty-first century to date for business – the global financial crisis (GFC). The GFC has been presented as an event that was set in 2008. However, its origins lie in the years before then and its impacts continue to roll out in the second half of the 2010s. The GFC is thus an ongoing issue that has a major impact on global markets, economies and social and political structures to this day and beyond.

After addressing the GFC, we focus on the broad range of new organizational forms and business models that have emerged since 2000. Some of these are variations on extant, historical forms, while some are new and innovative. Some you will recognize as the new 'mainstream' of international business, while others may at first seem surprising examples for an IB book – being illegal, morally questionable and subject to attempts to eliminate them from our world.

We introduce a disparate set of concepts and examples to prompt your thinking on how non-mainstream organizations and informal groups sit alongside, interact with, challenge or rely upon mainstream

IB organizations and models for their existence and for achievement of their particular goals.

Shifts in global economic power

One way to understand how the international business environment is changing is through observing shifts in the global economy in recent years. This is a common practice amongst economists and advisors to potential investors who use information about past and current trends in making decisions about where to direct their interest and where to locate investments. You will remember from Chapter 2 that, following a long period of nation state-centric perspectives on international trade, more recent thinking placed the company at the centre of IB theory and practice. When considered from a firm's point of view, countries can be evaluated as more or less promising locations for different kinds of IB activity.

A widely applied approach to classifying economies and markets is one based on the similarities they display with regard to a set of specific indicators, rather than on the basis of geographical proximity, as in the case of regional groupings. This takes the form of bringing a few countries together under a convenient to remember acronym. The most well-known example of this is the term 'BRICs'. Coined by Goldman Sachs' chief economist Jim O'Neill (2001) and first published in a paper entitled 'Building better global economic BRICs', the acronym refers to Brazil, Russia, India and China. According to O'Neill's forecast at the time, these four countries would collectively become increasingly more economically powerful. In 2003, this prediction was articulated in more specific terms in another paper, 'Dreaming with BRICs: The path to 2050' (Wilson and Purushothaman, 2003), which claimed that by 2050 the BRIC countries would be among the six largest economies in the world. They were forecast to overtake all historically most highly developed countries, other than the USA and Japan, in terms of their economic power. In O'Neill's view, the BRICs, regardless of their geographical and cultural differences, shared a number of characteristics that indicated that they had high potential for economic growth. These included: large populations, less developed economies than those of leading countries and an increasing level of market openness.

Over the next decade, the term BRICs became a 'brand' in its own right; not simply a descriptor used by investors and policymakers, but a lens through which they came to perceive emerging markets. Despite being criticized by some as no more than 'marketing hype', 'spin' or even 'nonsense' (Tett, 2010), the acronym has played an important role in both describing and driving a move away from the dominance of the west within the global economic system. Through influencing investors' behaviour, it has also given rise to new correlations in asset pricing. To ensure the continued success of the idea of the BRICs, Goldman Sachs regularly produced new reports, forecasts, books, videos and web tours, amounting to 21 products between 2001–2012. As Sum and Jessop (2015: 444) explain:

> The 'BRIC' imaginary continued to connect and circulate among economic strategists, investment consultants, sales teams etc. Its appeal derived not only from the projection of 'hope'/'strength' of the individual BRIC economies but also from their purported complementarity and profitability as an asset/investment group. Major international banks such as HSBC and other investment banks/ hedge funds began bundling stocks/shares/bonds and investing funds marketed as new financial instruments under the BRIC brand, including 4-Year MYR HSBC BRIC Markets Structured Investment, Templeton BRIC Fund (Singapore), and the iShares MSCI BRIC Index Fund.

While the idea of BRICs as emerging future economic powers continued to prevail for over a decade, another umbrella term was introduced a few years after the notion of BRICs was first articulated. O'Neill along with Anna Stupnytska (2005) predicted that a group they labelled 'N-11', also referred to as 'Next Eleven' economies would become powerful in the future. The list of N-11 countries consisted of Bangladesh, Egypt, Indonesia, Iran, Korea, Mexico, Nigeria, Pakistan, the Philippines, Turkey and Vietnam. The similarities between countries in this group were derived from variables including education and taxation. A few years later, Robert Ward from the Economist Intelligence Unit (EIU) proposed the acronym CIVETS, encompassing Colombia, Indonesia, Vietnam, Egypt, Turkey and South Africa. According to *The Economist* (2009), CIVETS was surfaced as a 'watchword' for studying the global economy in 2010. The term drew attention to six countries that, again, despite geographical and cultural dispersion, were all characterized by certain similarities, specifically, young populations, relatively stable and sophisticated financial systems, and the lack of overreliance on one particular sector of the economy. These features were argued to be reasons for investment in the countries as production locations and demand markets to be tapped into. CIVETS were popularized by former HSBC chief executive Michael Geoghegan, who enthused about their significance in early 2010 (Reuters, 2010). By 2012, the origins of CIVETS were being moved back in history to 2008 (Moore, 2012) and Standard & Poor's had a 'Civets 60' index, tracking the top 10 market performers in each country.

In 2013, as the BRIC economies appeared to exhibit less promising growth prospects, O'Neill yet again coined an acronym for the use of potential investors (Pan, 2013), this time by moving attention to four non-BRIC emerging economies with the highest population figures. The common features of the MINTs, i.e. Mexico, Indonesia, Nigeria and Turkey were big, growing and young populations. These were considered a particular 'asset' in terms of enabling future economic growth relative to developed countries, whose growth was seen as likely to be slowed down along with ageing and diminishing populations. Further, all MINT countries had the unique advantage of being located near other countries that offered large markets: the USA in the case of Mexico, China in proximity to Indonesia, the European Union close to Turkey, and potentially a range of African countries – provided their economies would experience strong development – in the case of Nigeria.

For a critical study of IB, the rise and fall of the acronyms discussed above, and their use by governments, banks, investors, MNCs, journalists and other interested parties, has a two-fold significance. On one hand, it helps us understand the recent and current dynamics within the global economy, especially in terms of the changing balance in economic power, and the possible direction in which this shift is likely to continue in years to come. In this sense, a basic familiarity with the economic and political situation in countries that have been included in the different groupings is useful for developing an understanding of important contemporary trends in IB, such as why – as discussed in Chapter 4 – the number of Chinese-based MNCs listed in the *Fortune 500* top 20 ranking by turnover has increased significantly over the last decade. On the other hand, it also points to the ways in which IB activity, as exemplified by the marketing of products offered to clients by global investment banks, can be triggered and developed through imaginative grouping and labelling of countries to create categories such as BRICs or MINTs that, as Elliott (2014) warns us, in the end of the day 'are only grouped together because they make a neat acronym'.

The global financial crisis

As previously stated, the beginnings of the global financial crisis can be traced to years before its culmination in 2008, with the collapse of the

American housing market and several financial institutions. On 9 August 2007, the French bank BNP Paribas made an announcement stating that it was freezing the assets of three of its hedge funds, barring investors from withdrawing cash from them. The main area of specialism of these funds was US mortgage debt. Several weeks later, in early September, UK bank Northern Rock sought support from the Bank of England as a result of its financial exposure.

The reason behind BNP Paribas' decision was the situation in the US sub-prime mortgage market (Kar-Gupta and Guernigou, 2007) – a market segment that consisted of customers who did not meet the usual criteria for being able to afford a mortgage. From its beginnings in the 1990s, the sub-prime market expanded rapidly in the early 2000s. In its early years, the higher interest rates paid by borrowers made this market segment attractive. However, from 2005, the number of people defaulting on their mortgages increased to such an extent that a lot of properties became available for sale at devalued prices, leading to a collapse of the housing market.

The problems at BNP Paribas and other institutions sent signals across the financial system that considerable losses were being incurred. While at the time it was not known what the exact amounts were and to what extent individual banks would be affected by the losses, trust between banking institutions had been damaged, adversely impacting banks' willingness to engage in business with one another. This was because the initial lenders on these sub-prime mortgages had sold on the debt that was then 'repackaged' into complex financial investment bundles and again sold on. As a result, financial institutions across the world had bought into this market without being aware of the degree of their exposure.

Throughout 2008, problems in the American housing market exacerbated, resulting in the American government bailing out two of the major players in the sub-prime mortgage market, Fannie Mae and Freddie Mac in early September. Later the same month, the investment bank Lehman Brothers filed for bankruptcy – the largest in history. What was particularly significant about this bankruptcy, is that in order for it to happen, the American government had to take a decision *not* to bail out Lehman Brothers. In the context of recent history within the banking sector – exemplified by the cases of Northern Rock, Fannie Mae and Freddie Mac – demonstrating that government would 'rescue' developed country banks experiencing serious financial difficulties, this was an unprecedented decision.

The practice of government bailouts is underpinned by a theory developed in economics that suggests that, due to their important position within the economy and their interconnectedness with other economic actors, certain organizations – especially within the financial sector – should be given financial protection by the government. This theory, whose major tenet is commonly referred to through the phrase 'too big to fail', contends that since the consequences of some corporations or banks going bankrupt would be detrimental to the whole economic system, the potential for this happening must be prevented through government intervention. To a critic, it might seem more logical that, rather than offering protection and allowing some firms to become so big and powerful that their failure would have far-reaching negative outcomes, government regulation should focus on making sure that no one company can become so big that its collapse threatens the whole economy. However, those who support the 'too big to fail' argument claim that size brings advantages in the form of economies of scale for businesses, leading to lower costs for them. These, in turn, can be passed onto their customers. As the 'too big to fail' theory was accepted and applied, business organizations and financial institutions in particular were allowed to grow in size and significance.

The specific reason given for the lack of government intervention in the case of Lehman Brothers was 'moral hazard'. Coined in behavioural economics, the concept of moral hazard refers to a situation where one party engages in risky behaviour because it knows that its costs will be borne by another party. A typical example of this at the level of an individual is when a person behaves in a less careful way, say, when they park their car if they know that it is fully insured and that the costs of any repairs to the vehicle incurred through their carelessness will be covered by the insurer. In the case of Lehman Brothers, the bank was considered by Hank Paulson, then US Secretary of the Treasury, to have acted in an irresponsible way through granting mortgage loans to borrowers who did not have full documentation normally required for ensuring that they would be able to afford repaying the loans.

A common explanation of why institutions like Lehman Brothers acted in a 'morally hazardous' way that in the end led to the GFC is that bankers' remunerations packages incentivized this kind of behaviour, and that they legitimized and fuelled executive greed. In particular, bankers' bonuses were not explicitly tied to aspects of their professional performance such as prudence or diligence, but to short-term profit. The enormous amounts paid to banking executives in the lead up to the GFC are illustrated by Roeder (2010: 31) stating that: 'By the time Lehman Brothers and Bear Stearns collapsed in 2008, the top five executives in both companies had collectively taken home $2.4 billion in salary, bonuses and stock since 2000'. This kind of explanation places the blame and responsibility for the crisis at the level of individuals employed by the banks. What also needs to be considered is the endemic culture and systemic weakness of the sector, specifically, the lack of adequate regulatory oversight.

Following the bankruptcy of Lehman Brothers, it became obvious that the banking sector was under threat. The crisis continued in the USA, and rapidly spread to other countries, including Iceland, Ireland and the UK. To ensure that financial systems in their countries would not collapse, in the final quarter of 2008 governments of European countries as well as the USA designated bailout packages: €480 billion in the case of Germany; €360 billion in the case of France; and £500 billion in the UK. Despite the bailouts of banks, the crisis – due to trade and financial interconnectedness – had begun to affect the global economy, driving it towards recession.

To prevent deepening of the recession, the G20 group – consisting of Argentina, Australia, Brazil, Canada, China, France, Germany, India, Indonesia, Italy, Japan, Mexico, Republic of Korea, Russia, Saudi Arabia, South Africa, Turkey, United Kingdom, United States and the European Union as a separate member – held a Summit on Financial Markets and World Economy in November 2008 in Washington, DC. As a result of the summit, G20 leaders agreed an Action Plan incorporating three key objectives: (1) Restoring global growth; (2) Strengthening the international financial system; (3) Reforming international financial institutions. The focus of the Action Plan was on strengthening transparency and accountability, and enhancing sound regulation of financial institutions, promoting integrity in financial markets, reinforcing international cooperation and reforming international financial institutions. An outcome of the summit was also the G20 Leaders' Declaration, offering the following explanation of the root causes of the crisis (OECD, 2008):

> During a period of strong global growth, growing capital flows, and prolonged stability earlier this decade, market participants sought higher yields without an adequate appreciation of the risks and failed to exercise proper due diligence. At the same time, weak underwriting standards, unsound risk management practices, increasingly complex and opaque financial products, and consequent excessive leverage combined to create vulnerabilities in the system. Policy-makers, regulators and supervisors, in some advanced countries, did not adequately appreciate and address the risks building up in financial markets, keep pace with financial innovation, or take into account the systemic ramifications of domestic regulatory actions. Major underlying factors to the

current situation were, among others, inconsistent and insufficiently coordinated macroeconomic policies, inadequate structural reforms, which led to unsustainable global macroeconomic outcomes. These developments, together, contributed to excesses and ultimately resulted in severe market disruption.

A period of reforms and actions followed, and slowly the economic situation began to improve. It is understood that the most difficult period of recession lasted in the USA from December 2007 to June 2009, and in the Eurozone from January 2008 to August 2009. However, in Europe in 2010 and 2011 a new stage of the crisis unfolded, marked by budgetary deficits, economic downturn, high unemployment and the Eurozone debt crisis – with Greece, as previously discussed, the most strongly affected European nation. At the beginning of 2012, economists expressed views that the Eurozone was undergoing a double-dip recession; Greece, Ireland and Portugal were considered to experience economic depression. The recession continued throughout 2012 and 2013. To bring governments' finances back on track, European societies were subjected to 'austerity' measures in line with IMF's recommendations for budget spending cuts affecting healthcare, pensions, disability payments, unemployment compensation and employment protections. In the circle of its proponents, referred to by the economist Rob Parenteau as 'austerians' (Krugman, 2012), these measures were believed to result in a return to economic stability and growth.

However, the 'austerian ideology' failed in practice and, as Paul Krugman (2015) noted, 'all of the economic research that allegedly supported the austerity push has been discredited. Widely touted statistical results were, it turned out, based on highly dubious assumptions and procedures – plus a few outright mistakes – and evaporated under closer scrutiny'. In 2016, economic commentators warned that, since the regulators have not reformed the banking system, another financial crisis and global economic crash were under way. In the words of the former Bank of England governor Sir Mervyn King, 'Another crisis is certain, and the failure … to tackle the disequilibrium in the world economy makes it likely that it will come sooner rather than later' (Marlow, 2016).

Alternative perspectives on IB activity

The mainstream literature on IB is focused primarily on discussion of examples that are accepted as being legal and as ethically legitimate or neutral. There has been some consideration in recent years of morally questionable activities, such as during the GFC as above, and case studies of illegal and unethical operations like the corporate collapses of WorldCom and Enron (cf. Healy and Palupu, 2008/2016). Here, we draw attention to a broad range of IB activities that fall outside of the mainstream. Some of these are entirely legal and place ethical considerations at the centre of their field, such as those of non-governmental organizations like Transparency International and War on Want. Others, as exemplified by Greenpeace and Sea Shepherd, are grounded in a proclaimed ethical stance, but have on occasion been deemed illegal in certain countries' courts of law. In addition, the nature of ethics is thrown open to question by those who argue for business activities based on alternative cultural perspectives on issues such as whaling. A third, more clearly defined category, is where international 'business' activities are generally accepted as both illegal and unethical across most if not all jurisdictions. These include drug trafficking and people smuggling.

Within the first type above, the activity of the organization is frequently targeted at identifying and exposing corrupt, unethical or illegal activities by other, often mainstream international businesses. Transparency International is a global coalition to fight corruption, 'shedding light on shady deals, weak enforcement of rules and other illicit practices that undermine good governments, ethical businesses and society at large' (Transparency International, 2015). The organization engages in collaboration with government, business and society representatives to bring about incremental change through a non-confrontational approach. Aiming specifically to change the values and practices of business, Transparency publishes a set of *Business Principles for Countering Bribery* (Transparency International, 2013).

War on Want is a UK-based international NGO aiming to 'achieve a vision of a just world ... [and] to fight against the root causes of poverty and human rights violation' (War on Want, 2016). While it is active across many fronts, its major impact on mainstream IB came when it motivated widespread critical response and action in the wake of the Rana Plaza tragedy in Bangladesh. As a result of public pressure, a number of retail MNCs committed to development of and became signatories to the *Bangladesh Accord on Fire and Building Safety* (the Bangladesh Accord) for better working conditions for garment workers in that country. By 2015, over 200 organizations had signed up to the Accord, including major MNCs such as Adidas, Benetton, Carrefour, and Marks and Spencer (bangladeshaccord.org, 2015). Oxfam International also gathered support for the Accord. Formed in 1995 from a coalition of NGOs, this organization describes itself as 'part of a global movement, campaigning with others … to end unfair trade rules, demand better health and education services for all, and to combat climate change' (Oxfam International, 2016).

The second type of activity shares many similarities with the first, but is conducted by organizations that are willing to push up to, and sometimes beyond, the boundaries of legality in jurisdictions where they act. Greenpeace describes itself as 'an independent global campaigning organization that acts to change attitudes and behaviour, to protect and conserve the environment' (Greenpeace, 2015). While these aims will be seen as perfectly reasonable and justifiable, the means by which the organization promotes its message have been found to be in breach of standards and law on more than one occasion (cf. RNZ, 2012). In September 2015, Greenpeace celebrated victory over the Shell company when the latter abandoned its Arctic oil exploration drilling programme (Glaser, 2015). While Shell claimed that the discoveries of oil were not commercially viable and withdrawal was a purely commercial decision, Greenpeace's intervention included disrupting Shell's operations by direct actions, some of which had been deemed illegal in court and were decried by business commentators (e.g. Clemente, 2015). Similarly, the Sea Shepherd group acknowledges on its own website that its members were found guilty in a court of law, but then uses this guilt under one nation's law to support its own ethical stance on the issue of whaling (Sea Shepherd, 2015).

The IB activities we outline above may be viewed as legal, or as pushing the boundaries of legality from a particular moral standpoint. However, there are others that clearly lie in the domain of illegality and are also judged by the vast majority as being unethical and immoral. At the same time, they are both international in nature and are frequently organized along business lines. These include trafficking in illegal drugs. A 2011 UN study found that revenues from transnational drug trafficking and organized crime in the first decade of the century constituted on average $650 billion per year, equivalent to 1.5% of global GDP (UNODC, 2011). The report noted that as the trade was increasing, by 2009 these revenues were likely to have been around $870 billion, of which some $580 billion – 1% of global GDP – was likely laundered through the global financial system. In Australia, concerns have been expressed that this type of money has been invested into a booming housing market (Aston, 2016).

Similar to drug trafficking, human trafficking is an international activity that generates vast revenues, often laundered through legitimate financial institutions. In addition, this form of criminal activity frequently feeds directly into another business form that many find morally questionable – legal prostitution. A UN Factsheet (UNODC, undated) estimated that in Europe alone criminals were generating around €2.5 billion per year from sexual exploitation and forced labour from this trafficking. In countries as far apart as Australia (Duff, 2015) and Germany (Spiegel Online International, 2013) there have been reports on how young women are trafficked and trapped into legal brothels, from which authorities often seem either unable or unwilling to extract them.

We have introduced you to this diverse and seemingly unrelated set of 'international business' activities to prompt your thinking beyond the mainstream and, with examples, to demonstrate that notions of mainstream/alternative, legal/illegal and moral/immoral are not always clear-cut and easily separated.

The Internet era of IB

All internationally focused organizations – and most domestic ones – now rely upon Internet technologies to conduct business. These include public, private and not-for-profit organizations, along with the criminal networks we discuss above. In addition, new types of 'international business' have emerged that have drawn on these technologies from the outset and are dependent upon them. As with the examples in the previous section, these range along continua of legal/illegal and ethical/unethical, where both categories may be debatable across different national contexts. They also sit in a variety of relations with mainstream IB actors and activities. There are many types of new organization with which you will be familiar that are built around Internet-based business models. These include Google – incorporated into the new parent company Alphabet in 2015 – Baidu, Facebook, Tencent and Twitter. New ideas and company names emerge regularly, so we cannot claim to be up to date as you read. However, we wish to raise and discuss issues that are transferable to other examples.

The first example is one where 'traditional' businesses have adopted the power of the Internet to improve their efficiency. 'E-procurement' has been adopted by different organizational types – from public sector authorities to MNCs. The aim of e-procurement is to open up new ways of purchasing products and services through seeking prices and tenders through the Internet. This allows for increasing the geographic spread of the procurement net whilst reducing dramatically the transaction time. For example, established in 2000 by 13 major global airlines, Aeroxchange now boasts a global network of airlines and aerospace suppliers that use e-procurement to buy and sell all aircraft components, from the smallest of parts to jet engines, and both new and refurbished (cf. Aeroxchange.com, 2015). One particular form of e-procurement that offers cost saving potential to buyers is the 'reverse auction'. Here, the purchaser publishes information on their needs and prospective suppliers bid against each other to put forward the lowest price to meet the specification. In contrast to submission of sealed bids by the suppliers, this is a dynamic process that places power firmly in the hands of the procuring organization. Since suppliers see their competitors' offers during the bidding, they must decide how low they are prepared to drive their own price. In the international arena, such an auction can only be conducted online.

As existing firms use the Internet for innovative ways of doing business, new types of organization emerge that employ and rely on Internet tools from the beginning. These businesses frequently mobilize and coordinate global bodies of largely self-employed individuals, seeking to supplant existing organizations in the same market. Examples here include Airbnb and Uber. The first is a web-based MNC that enables individuals to list, find and rent accommodation. The second is an American MNC that developed the idea of allowing prospective travellers to use their smartphones to submit details of a journey, to which Uber drivers can respond. Uber relies upon a body of self-employed drivers using their own vehicles, where the price of the service is determined by a complex algorithm that takes account of the demand for journeys and availability of drivers at a given time in a certain area. While the brand has spread to over 50 countries, the business model has been accepted as legal in some cities and illegal in others. The ethics of Uber is subject to considerable debate and controversy across the world, even where it is legal (cf. Segall, 2014). The organization promotes the notion of freedom of choice for both the customer and the driver (Uber.com, 2016a). However, there have been complaints from both sides, with drivers themselves raising concerns about too many and low-quality drivers and having to work 'silly hours' to earn a living (Knowles, 2015). In addition, Uber drivers have been subjected to fines, intimidation and, in some places, physical assault from 'legitimate' taxi drivers (cf. Malalo and Jorgic, 2016).

In addition to new Internet models of business organization, there is an entirely new class of 'anti-business' activism that is conducted seemingly without organization, that will often claim a moral standpoint, will on some occasions remain within the law but sometimes resorts to illegal actions. While these groups may claim to be standing against governments and MNCs in particular, they rely upon both the tools and resources of IB to promulgate their message. Here, we group those that are recognized by names like The Occupy Movement and Anonymous.

The Occupy Movement grew internationally from the Occupy Wall Street movement of 2011, itself inspired by earlier social uprisings against dominant power structures, notably the so-called Arab Spring that bloomed first in Tunisia in 2010. These movements have no identifiable 'management' team, no 'head office' and no formal structures, yet have succeeded in coordinating and mobilizing large groups of individuals, primarily in protest against prevailing social, economic and political conditions. While the Arab Spring was mostly a stance against political regimes, the Occupy Movement was targeted at the financial institutions that were considered to lie at the root of the GFC, and whose senior officials appeared to have remained relatively unscathed by it. Its message was one of critique of growing socio-economic fragmentation and wealth accumulation by the richest 1% of the population under the banner, 'We are the 99%'. From its origins in New York, Occupy spread rapidly across the globe into every continent. Although the movement was intended to be non-violent, there were some incidences of violence both by and against members. One critical comment – that is worth considering also in relation to any business activity – came from nonviolent theorist, Dr Gene Sharp (2011). He noted that since the movement had no clear objective, something they could actually achieve by their actions, then simply occupying a space would be unlikely to bring about any change to prevailing socio-economic conditions. In the end, this appears to have been the case, as 'occupy' faded from memory as the most used word on the English-speaking Internet in 2011 (*The Telegraph*, 2011).

The Occupy Movement may have had little apparent impact, particularly on business practice. However, another form of web-based activism has had very clear repercussions for some MNCs: the Anonymous group, a loose international network where members appear in public wearing Guy Fawkes masks. Anonymous started out with some fairly innocuous stunts, but moved on to claim responsibility for 'distributed denial-of-service' (DDoS) attacks on the computer networks of government, religious and corporate organizations, including those of global financial institutions. While the group has been celebrated by some as 'freedom fighters' and 'digital Robin Hoods', others have described members as 'cyber terrorists' (cf. Rawlinson and Peachey, 2012). However you may view them, the Anonymous group earned the accolade of being listed among *Time* magazine's most influential people of 2012 (Gellman, 2012).

The final type of international organization that we wish to highlight is one that engages in extremism for idealistic ends but that relies upon IB tools and transactions for disseminating its message and for its fundraising. Here, we point to ISIS and the so-called Islamic State.

These are not IB organizations, but are linked to the IB world in two very different ways. First, as with the examples above, they rely on the web-based communication media of business to spread their message and gain attention outside their immediate sphere of geographic control. Second, and of particular interest, they depend upon trade of commodities, including crude oil (Faulconbridge and Saul, 2015) and cultural antiquities (Shabi, 2015), in international markets to generate funds to again engage in IB markets – through black markets and corrupt officials (*The Economist*, 2015) – to purchase armaments.

Beyond international – the age of extra-territoriality

Some of the examples we discuss in this chapter raise questions about how international businesses and counter-organizations attempt to de-territorialize themselves, to be seen as everywhere, to base themselves in 'the cloud', or even to seek to be found nowhere. An example of being omnipresent is Uber. While the origins of the business can be traced to one city location, San Francisco, it has achieved a state of extra- or de-territoriality evidenced by its web presence. Searching for the highest-level website – www.uber.com – from our writing location, we find that the organization does not explicitly reveal its geographic placement. On the other hand, our location in Australia is immediately identified, and we are presented with the banner that reads, 'Uber is in Brisbane and 405 other cities worldwide'. As prospective customers, we are tracked and pinned down, while the business remains in the cloud, or at least not tied to one place. At the time of writing, Uber's careers page for 'open roles' (not drivers) advertised positions for: accounts executives in the USA and UK, accounting managers in India and the Philippines, business systems developers in the Netherlands, and marketing managers in Beijing (Uber.com, 2016b).

Such internationalization and resultant cross-cultural operations may be seen as a positive move in a globalized world. However, one way that many MNCs have exploited their extra- and de-territoriality is in facilitating tax avoidance, or in some cases tax evasion – the former being legal but morally questionable and the latter illegal. The issue of morality and tax avoidance has been raised as one that might be considered in, yet has been largely absent from, the academic literature on 'corporate social responsibility' (CSR) (cf. Dowling, 2014). In his book chapter on 'Tax avoidance, tax evasion, money laundering and the problem of "offshore"', Alldridge (2015) discusses the distinctions between the first two, but also the blurred line that separates them. In a comprehensive analysis of the complexities of company tax, he highlights specific issues related to MNCs' multi-territoriality that enable them to avoid being pinned to a single location for tax purposes. He explains how firms use their multiple locations and the separateness of their subsidiaries in these to transfer profits between them to minimize their tax liabilities in high taxation nations and, hence, across the business. He also draws attention to the issue of 'transfer pricing' addressed in detail by Sikka and Willmott (2010). Here, subsidiaries buy and sell assets inside the MNC, not at market value but at whatever price – whether ultra-inflated or near-zero – that will again impact the balance sheet to minimize tax liabilities across the organization.

In addition to discussion of MNC activities, there is a critical debate of alleged government action by new global economic powers, particularly China, in extra-territorial land 'grabs' in Africa and other poorer parts of the world. A UN report (Cotula et al., 2009) refers to Chinese land deals as, first, an investment opportunity and, second and less so, as a contributor to food security. The UN acknowledges the lack of accurate information and data about African land deals and one source (Smith, 2009) speaks of how 'a million Chinese farmers have joined the rush to Africa'. At the same time, another commentator (Brautigam, 2015) argues that most of the claims of massive land acquisitions are over-inflated and not to be believed. Similarly, a Swedish NGO (Olsson, 2012) accuses western media sources of engaging in wilful accusations of extensive Chinese 'neo-colonialism' when the truth is one of small-scale agricultural collaboration. Whatever the reality of the current situation, we can be fairly certain that, as populations continue to grow and as climate change impacts water and food security, the international business of land will become of major significance for all nations.

Secrecy, information and misinformation

Many of the activities we have referred to above are kept secret and subject to non-disclosure by both businesses and governments, despite the efforts of organizations like Transparency International and calls for reform over decades. As individual governments and the G7/G8 have moved slowly towards incremental change, the level of protest and rate of change have been impacted in dramatic fashion in 2016 by release of the so-called Panama Papers (cf. Harding, 2016). Containing some 2.6 terabytes of information leaked from Panamanian law firm Mossack Fonseca, these papers represent the largest-ever illicit disclosure of computerized data, far exceeding Wikileaks and all similar 'whistle-blower' releases. Both the content of these papers and the manner of their release are of interest in the field of IB. First, in terms of content, the papers revealed the alleged involvement of tens of thousands of businesses and individuals across the globe in complex arrangements for unethical tax avoidance and illegal tax evasion. Politicians from countries ranging from the UK to Russia were implicated in various ways, while those forced to resign almost immediately included the Icelandic Prime Minister and the President of Transparency International in Chile (Slattery, 2016).

While the papers themselves exposed dubious tax linkages across a broad range of individuals and organizations within a complex global web, the analysis of the leaked documents and the manner of their release provide evidence of another new transnational organizational form. In order to gain maximum exposure and impact from the documents, while acknowledging that they emerged as a result of a criminal act, their analysis and initial partial release was coordinated by a multinational grouping. This included the International Consortium of Investigative Journalists (ICIJ), *The Guardian*, BBC and other outlets with global reach. As we write, the initial public impact of the papers has receded behind issues including Brexit and the US Presidential election. However, the investigations, prosecutions and impacts on IB organizations and activities will roll on for years to come. Even though the documents emerged as a result of a criminal act, the Danish government decided in September 2016 to purchase information on implicated Danish citizens from an anonymous source. This decision was described as 'deeply reprehensible' by an opposition spokesperson (BBC, 2016).

Those individuals and organizations that have been exposed in the Panama Papers may have felt secure in hiding their unethical and, in many cases illegal, activities on what they considered secure servers, with legal protection. However, it has been shown that the actions of an individual with support from a network of equally secure, but more reliable, resources can break through the deceptions and layers of misinformation behind which major public figures hide their tax activities. The example of the Panama Papers indicates that, in the Internet era, everything is connected and anonymity is nowhere guaranteed anymore.

Tax, business and society

In this chapter, we have raised the topics of tax avoidance and tax evasion several times. We have highlighted that the first is legal, but morally questionable, while the second is illegal. Questions regarding tax evasion should then become relatively simple to answer – it is against the law, so those that engage in it should be prosecuted. However, as the example of the Panama Papers shows, individuals and organizations will go to great lengths, operating across national boundaries and legal jurisdictions to conceal what is in effect criminal activity. In this, they are often assisted, whether knowingly or otherwise, by a range of actors and structures. There are lawyers and accountants that are implicated in enabling clients to engage in tax evasion. At the same time, contemporary Internet banking systems make it simpler for money to be transferred between multiple accounts and to become virtually untraceable.

While tax evasion can be prosecuted under law, when uncovered, tax avoidance is perfectly legal. Most individuals and organizations will happily look to 'optimize' their tax liabilities. Firms will do so using a range of mechanisms, including transfer pricing, as described earlier. However, critics of corporate tax avoidance argue that many MNCs – and wealthy individuals – pay little or no tax in any country through careful manipulation of legal processes. They point out that ordinary citizens of the countries where vast profits and earnings are generated do not have access to such opportunities. This means that the burden of taxation is increased for those that must pay, while those that can avoid doing so take advantage of the infrastructure, services and other social goods funded by those that pay.

In the following chapter, we develop discussion of individuals and IB, and outline an example of how the wealthy might use their position to benefit poorer members of society. Here, however, we put to you the question that critical commentators ask – should individuals be able to accumulate such wealth and choose where to spend on social good? Or, should they be taxed at a suitable rate that enables government and public sector bodies to decide and spend? In addition, we draw attention to the maxim employed by investigative individuals who seek to uncover and expose cases of both tax avoidance and evasion – 'follow the money'.

Conclusions

In this chapter, we discussed how since 2000 there have been fundamental changes in the landscape of international business environment. We highlighted how shifts in relative economic significance between nation states, moving power away from western nations, were identified. These were labelled using acronyms that, while making it easy to remember which countries were being considered, may be seen as choices of convenience for the sake of the name.

We then proceeded to discuss the major event of the twenty-first century to date, in terms of impact on the global economy, namely the GFC. In addressing the origins, immediate impacts, roll-on effects and the different interpretations of the crisis, we demonstrated that this was not a single event at a point in time. Neither is it open to clear analysis in order to attribute blame and show how such an event can be avoided in future. Rather, we see the GFC as a phenomenon that must be examined from multiple perspectives to gain insight into its possible causes and an understanding of its continuing impacts.

We outlined and discussed a broad range of business, organizational and informal groups whose activities are either designed around or are dependent upon new Internet technologies. Some of these are formal and legitimate organizations while others are not businesses and some undertake activities that are clearly anti-business, or anti-dominant political and ideological forms. Our purpose in doing this has been to challenge your thinking on what might be understood as 'international business', and to highlight how groups and practices that are not normally included in the IB literature both draw upon business practices for their own ends, and can impact mainstream IB activities by their actions.

Finally, we provided a brief expansion of discussion on the topics of tax avoidance and tax evasion. We clarified the legal difference between these, but pointed out that both are morally questionable. We offered some ideas on how to critically assess businesses and individuals in regard to the status of their tax payments and the impacts of this on broader society.

In the final two chapters of our book, we offer a number of ways to further understand the dynamics of international business, with the intention of enabling you to undertake critical analysis of IB practices and situations in which you are interested or directly involved.

Questions

1. Investigate and compare how executives in the banking sectors of the UK and Iceland at the time of the GFC in 2008 have been treated by their respective political and legal systems over the following decade. What are the implications of differences in terms of public confidence in the two banking sectors?

2. What has been the manner of market entry and growth of Uber in a country of your choice? How was this enabled or blocked at the outset by existing legal frameworks? What has been the subsequent impact on 'traditional' taxi service providers?
3. Select an aspect of the Panama Papers case that is of interest to you and that has been subject to investigation and reporting in the media, political and legal sectors of a country of your choice. What has been the impact of the investigation and reporting on the individuals and organizations that are their subjects?

Further reading

Pitesa, M. and Thau, S. (2013) 'Masters of the universe: How power and accountability influence self-serving decisions under moral hazard', *Journal of Applied Psychology*, 98(3): 550–558. Available at: https://hal.archives-ouvertes.fr/file/index/docid/814565/filename/pitesa_thau_JAP_2013.pdf (accessed 22 September 2016).

Shy, O. (2016) 'Fed's focus on "too big to fail" won't save taxpayers from next bank bailout', *The Conversation*, 9 July. Available at: http://theconversation.com/feds-focus-on-too-big-to-fail-wont-save-taxpayers-from-next-bank-bailout-61884 (accessed 22 September 2016).

Sikka, P. and Willmott, H. (2013) 'The tax avoidance industry: Accountancy firms on the make', *Critical Perspectives on International Business*, 9: 415–443. Available at: http://repository.essex.ac.uk/8128/1/WP2013-2_Corporate_Governance.pdf (accessed 22 September 2016).

6

People in International Business

██████ Introduction

The focus of this chapter is on how organizations operating within the international business environment influence and are influenced by people. Referring here to 'people', we mean a variety of individuals and groups affecting and affected by IB: from employees and managers to consumers and suppliers, local communities and society at large. Our intention is to move the discussion of people in IB beyond considerations that would traditionally fall under the discipline of Human Resource Management (HRM), and that would deal only with those directly employed by IB companies. Since IB activity is based on a complex set of relations with different parties both within the firm and outside it, we hope to inspire you to think of people in IB in a broader sense, and to reflect on the ways in which MNCs and other organizations within the international arena interact with and affect the lives of a wide range of stakeholders.

As explained earlier, we view IB through the lens of stakeholder theory, which states that a firm's responsibility is not limited to its shareholders but extends over all constituencies that have a stake in the firm (Freeman, 1984). When considered from this perspective, firms are expected to engage in value creation as 'a joint process that makes each primary stakeholder better off' (Freeman et al., 2007: 52), without the need to compromise some parties' interests over those of others. In this chapter, we draw on a number of relevant theories and concepts, as well as a selection of recent examples from IB practice to draw your attention to the dynamic relationship between the firm and its stakeholders, and between different categories of stakeholders. We conclude by reflecting on the extent to which stakeholder interests are and could be met through IB activities.

Staffing policy and HRM practices in the international organization

The international organization faces choices regarding whom to employ in its worldwide operations and within the separate country markets in which it does business. With regard to the cultural background of recruited management staff members, three general approaches can be identified: ethnocentric, polycentric and geocentric. The first of these relates to a policy of employing home-country nationals in key management positions in all markets. Historically, this approach was popular with firms that sought to maintain a strong identity and company focus. The popularity of the ethnocentric approach has faded in response to criticism of cultural myopia and the lack of career development opportunities for host country staff. The second approach is one of employing host country staff in senior posts. Here, from the point of view of the organization's top management, there are advantages of local knowledge, but there may be barriers to wider communication and transfer within the firm, due to language and other differences. The geocentric approach, that can be related to identification with cultural diversity, involves the firm in selecting the best possible people for all management positions across the organization, regardless of nationality. It is worth noting that there is an underlying assumption that, no matter which of these three approaches is adopted, profit and other benefits to the firm are prioritized over whatever advantages and disadvantages might accrue to the individual and to the society in which the company operates. In the field of healthcare in the UK, for example, a shortage of suitably qualified staff has led to the active recruitment of nursing and other staff from Africa, without regard for the resultant chronic shortage of trained staff to provide an adequate level of care and, in countries such as Malawi, with their own problems of endemic HIV and malaria (cf. Vidal, 2015).

Beyond nationality, staffing decisions within firms require consideration of a broader range of issues, since individual countries and governments often place restrictions on access by, and employment of, non-nationals. Such policies can be either universal or selective. For example, within the European Union, there is a high degree of labour mobility amongst most member states, with legislation to guarantee that citizens of the majority of EU countries are not disadvantaged when applying for jobs in countries other than that of their origin. At the same time, employment of non-EU citizens is restricted and controlled by work permits and visas granted on the basis of consideration of the individual case. Overall, the recent trend has been towards liberalization of rules governing international movement of labour that, in turn, has resulted in increased numbers of 'individuals who personally take charge of their careers without the direct support of an organization' (Cerdin and Selmer, 2014: 1281). These so called 'self-initiated expatriates' (SIEs) are often presented in the academic literature on international careers as those who pursue unrestricted, self-chosen and 'boundaryless careers' (DeFillippi and Arthur, 1994) directed at professional advancement. However, as Loacker and Śliwa (2016: 657) argue, since these kinds of professionals take on themselves some of the risks and uncertainties that previously would have been taken care of by the employing organization, they often find themselves 'in a position "in between" choice and necessity, and privilege and disadvantage'. In this sense, some dimensions of the international movement of workers might be seen as creating greater advantages for the organization in the IB environment rather than for its potential employees.

At the time of writing this book, the notion of international mobility of workers is receiving a lot of attention in the context of UK's referendum decision to leave the European Union. The Brexit vote provides an example of society's influence on the IB environment, an issue we discuss in more detail in Chapter 7. In terms of considering questions about employment viewed from an international perspective, with 3 million EU citizens living in the UK (over 2 million of whom are in employment) and 1.3 million Britons living in EU countries outside the UK, the Brexit vote has given rise to unsettling questions. Will all these expatriates across Europe be allowed to remain in their countries of residence? Will they be able to continue being legally employed, or will they require employment visas and work permits? For SIEs living and working in the UK, Brexit creates an incentive, or in some cases a perceived need, to relocate to a different country. For companies employing many non-UK citizens in Britain, it provides a reason to move operations to other European countries. An example of this is the cosmetics manufacturer Lush that decided to offer its non-British employees (around 500 people) from the company's operations in Poole, UK, the possibility to move to a new factory in Düsseldorf, Germany. In the words of the co-founder, Mark Constantine: 'all those people have been told they're not welcome and not wanted by people in Poole' (Constantine, 2016). The Lush case shows how the dynamics of IB environment impact the stability of companies' operations, and in consequence the stability of their employees' jobs.

Consumers in IB

Questions regarding the engagement of businesses operating internationally with their consumers are typically addressed by the academic literature on international marketing (e.g. Alon et al., 2016; Baack et al., 2012; Hollensen, 2016) and – in practice – by companies' international marketing activities. Here, we consider an alternative perspective on international business – one that is grounded in Aristotle's *phronēsis*. We explore IB-related issues through the lens of a phronetic inquiry, and an understanding of international marketing in relation to Aristotle's virtue ethics. Many authors have drawn attention to the need for organizations, selling goods and services in the international arena, to behave ethically. Murphy (1999) proposes that in the context of international marketing, ethical organizations should be characterized by five core virtues, namely: integrity, fairness, trust, respect and empathy. While we do not have the space here to offer a detailed discussion of international marketing, we present three aspects of the relationship between international businesses, especially MNCs, and their consumers: marketing to the poor; marketing of products through ways that reinforce race-related stereotypes; and ethical consumption. We use the first two as illustrations of the impacts of companies operating internationally on their consumers, and the third to demonstrate the influence of consumers on the practices of firms engaged in IB.

Selling to the poor

In recent years, MNCs have directed more and more of their marketing efforts towards low-income consumers, sometimes labelled the 'base-of-the-pyramid' or 'bottom'-market. Within these market segments, customers not only have a very low level of disposable income, but are also limited in terms of a range of life opportunities, such as education, political power and access to markets. The World Bank (1990) refers to these segments of the population as the 'marginal poor': people whose economic resources are too low for them to enjoy 'marginally comfortable' lifestyles, although they might have sufficient food to protect themselves and their families from starvation, and perhaps even a small income. The 'marginally poor' often live in developing countries – those locations where, to take advantage of low labour costs, MNCs would traditionally concentrate the 'supply' part of their global value chains. Here, they might typically locate their manufacturing of products and operations of call centres serving customers in western countries. However, as high- and mid-income markets become saturated, MNCs have begun to sell goods and services in places where, due to the limited purchasing power of local populations, potential marketing activities were previously considered 'unprofitable' (Prahalad, 2005).

Proponents of the recent 'marketing to the poor' trend argue that, thanks to MNCs' entry into the low-income markets, those who in the past were excluded from the benefits of economic development are now given the opportunity to participate in the advantages afforded by capitalism. Further, they suggest that as a result of their marketing activities in poverty-stricken regions of the world – and especially through investing in future consumption possibilities – MNCs contribute to poverty alleviation in these locations (e.g. Lodge and Wilson, 2006; Rangan et al., 2007). Critics, on the other hand, warn that as MNCs target the world's poor with their products and services, these consumers are at risk of greater exploitation. They argue that MNCs' profit generation can be augmented as a result of buyers' lack of education and other resources (e.g. Klein, 2002).

Discussing ethical dilemmas associated with MNCs' involvement in such impoverished market segments, authors in the field of business ethics have stressed the importance of MNCs operating in the low-income market grounding their activities in a strong normative ethical framework. An example of such a framework is offered by Santos and Laczniak (2009) who put forward the 'integrative justice model' (IJM). This aims to increase the level of fairness and equity in economic transactions with impoverished consumers, and illustrates what 'fair and non-exploitative' micro-marketing engagement with the poor might look like. In Santos and Laczniak's (2009: 5) view, when engaging with poor and disadvantaged consumers, firms' behaviour should have the following five characteristics:

1. Authentic engagement with consumers, particularly impoverished ones, with nonexploitative intent;
2. Cocreation of value with customers, especially those who are impoverished or disadvantaged;
3. Investment in future consumption without endangering the environment;
4. Interest representation of all stakeholders, particularly impoverished customers; and
5. Focus on long-term profit management rather than on short-term profit maximization.

In practice, following the principles of 'fair and nonexploitative' marketing has implications for all aspects of marketing activity. It requires rethinking the market research instruments applied prior to deciding which products and services to sell, and a change in the mindset behind wishing to make profit from selling to 'bottom-of-the-pyramid' consumers. This might involve a move away from using standard market research surveys to establish which products and services consumers are not using and, therefore, which ones could be introduced to them. It might also require withdrawal from marketing campaigns aimed at generating a 'customer need' for a specific product/service. Rather, MNCs might send marketers to impoverished communities to spend time amongst the people – to find out how they live, and what products and services might meet their existing needs. These may contribute to improving the quality of their lives, and provide investment to ensure such communities can achieve long-term, sustainable socio-economic development. They may also support an increase in consumption in the future. While this way of engaging with the world's poor by MNCs would not be free from ethical dilemmas and challenges, it would align with the objective of making a positive change to the lives of impoverished consumers rather than merely exploiting them.

Problematic marketing practices

The influence of IB firms' marketing activities on consumers can sometimes be viewed as problematic, not necessarily because of their economically exploitative nature, but because of the socio-cultural effects of the marketing campaign used to promote a given product. One example of this is the way in which skin-whitening products are marketed in countries such as India or Thailand. In 2013, Citra, the Thai subsidiary of the MNC Unilever, launched a competition for customers in Thailand. Female students were asked to send photographs of themselves wearing a university uniform and carrying a bottle of the MNC's skin-whitening product called Citra Pearly White UV body lotion (Hodal, 2013). The person who appeared on the winning photograph was promised a university scholarship of 100,000 baht (£2,000) sponsored by the company. In the TV and YouTube advert accompanying the competition, two female students were cast, one lighter- and one darker-skinned. Both were asked a question by the presenter about what could make them 'outstanding' as students. While the darker-skinned student did not give an answer, the lighter-skinned one – described by the presenter as 'beautiful' – answered that Citra products could help her become outstanding. The advertisement attracted criticism for implying a link between intelligence and a lighter skin colour, and for drawing on age-long positive connotations of light skin in upper class Thai society. The advert was subsequently withdrawn and Unilever – that claimed not to have wished to suggest racial discrimination – apologized for 'misunderstandings' that stemmed from the campaign.

The case of Unilever's Citra advertising in Thailand is representative of the situation across south-east Asia, where skin-lightening products, such as cosmetics, diet supplements and pills are commonly marketed to customers. The products are typically advertised by pale-skinned celebrities and models. Adverts tend to imply a link between a lighter skin colour and various positive characteristics, such as 'loveliness' of women's personality, 'handsomeness' of men's appearance and overall 'success' in life. In India, the fairness cream industry is estimated to be worth around $450 mn (Banerji, 2016). The majority of skin-whitening cosmetics – including the most popular line branded 'Fair and Lovely' – are sold by Hindustan Unilever: again, a subsidiary of the British–Dutch consumer goods MNC. The industry justifies its existence based on the argument that there is a demand for skin-lightening products, that businesses are prepared to fulfil this demand, and that customers' rights are protected by the freedom to choose whether or not to buy and use such products. Taking a broader socio-cultural view of the phenomenon of marketing skin-lightening products to non-white customers, however, makes it impossible to ignore the fact that in developing such products, firms exploit historically conditioned racial prejudices and stereotypes. At the same time, the proliferation of such products on the market means that the aspiration to have lighter skin – rooted in the assumption that having white skin is 'better' and more desirable than having dark skin – continues to be seen as normal and unproblematic where they are marketed. In this way, racial prejudices and stereotypes are further reinforced. At the individual level, this brings negative consequences for the self-esteem of people, especially the young, with darker skin in Asian and African countries. At the level of society, it reinforces race-based divisions and inequalities. In addition, it may cause health risks, as some of the products have been reported to contain toxic chemicals and steroids that have been linked to a range of negative side effects in users (Goldstein, 2012).

The example of marketing skin-lightening products in countries such as India and Thailand by MNCs demonstrates the complexity of the ethical issues within the relationship between IB companies and their consumers. Below, we discuss another aspect of this relationship, with reference to 'ethical consumption'.

Ethical consumption

Having evolved from 'green consumerism', ethical consumerism – as an area of research and an approach to consumption practice by individuals and groups – has developed as a response to perceived social impacts of contemporary patterns of consumption. The literature on their negative consequences has pointed to how growth in consumption levels results in depleting natural resources and disrupting environmental equilibrium at a global level. Writers discuss the increased inequalities between those who are able to access certain goods and services, and those who cannot, and how this jeopardizes the possibilities of building sustainable communal life.

The proponents of ethical consumption point to IB and MNCs as key forces behind the spread of consumerism across the world. They see them as the most significant actors driving global consumption, with little consideration of ethics, sustainability and their overall impact on different stakeholder groups, including future generations. Those researching ethical consumption in relation to IB and the operations of MNCs have focused on topics such as: fair trade, labour standards and consumer boycotts. Consumer groups have called for MNCs to engage with their suppliers, such as coffee or fruit growers, on a fair trade basis, and to follow industry-level codes of conduct when employing workers in different countries across the world. Their objective has been to seek improvement in the economic situation and the working conditions of people in developing countries. Consumer boycotts as a form of pressure on MNCs have been underpinned by a range of concerns – from animal welfare and genetic modification of food to unethical corporate behaviour. In many cases, these have proved effective as a means of applying pressure to companies. In 2012, in response to a report and boycott call by the Campaign for Safe Cosmetics (CSC), the American cosmetics giant Johnson & Johnson changed the formula of all its baby products. The firm removed a formaldehyde-releasing preservative; a harmful chemical linked to certain types of cancer in humans. Another example of an MNC's change in their IB practices as a result of consumer boycott is the case of the garment manufacturer Fruit of the Loom. The largest student boycott in history was initiated in 2009 by United Students Against Sweatshops in response to the closure of the company's Honduran factory after its workers unionized. As a result of the campaign, 96 US colleges and 10 British universities terminated contracts with Fruit of the Loom, costing the firm $50 million. In 2010 the MNC re-opened the factory, re-employed all its 1,200 workers, restored all union rights and awarded workers \$2.5 million in compensation. Such examples highlight the complexity of the relationships between different stakeholders in the IB environment. MNCs affect consumers across the world, whereas consumers can affect both the activities of MNCs and, at the same time, the workers who are directly involved in the production of goods and service delivery by MNCs.

We return to these multi-directional impacts between different IB stakeholders later in this chapter. Below, we put forward some ideas regarding the relationship between IB companies and another stakeholder group: those employed in global supply chains.

Employment in global supply chains

As companies have moved production away from their country of origin, and have developed global supply chains whose control and ownership structures are complex, pertinent questions have emerged about how to ensure decent working conditions in global supply chains (Donaghey et al., 2014). For many, the subject of employment within global supply chains brings to mind sweatshops, unsafe working environments and poor working conditions suffered by workers. Sometimes these workers are reported to be children or individuals who are forced to work against their will. They are considered likely to be employed in low-paid jobs. Such jobs, at best, allow them to survive but with little chance of building sustainable livelihoods. At worst, their workplaces frequently become locations where tragedy occurs. An example of one of the most widely reported tragedies, and a story that epitomizes the direct negative impact of MNCs' operations on those who work in global supply chains is that of 18 suicides attempted at Foxconn – China's biggest factory located in Shenzhen in the south of the country. Fourteen of the involved workers died, all of whom were less than 25 years old. The company is part of the global electronic industry and is best known as contractor to Apple, producing iPhones and iPads marketed for the California-based MNC. The industry has been blamed for relying on 'what is effectively a human battery-farming system' (Chakrabortty, 2013) that involves the employment of young, poor migrant workers from rural China. On relocation from home, they are accommodated in crowded dormitories and spend their days in large workhouses, subjected to demands to work long hours. It is quite common for these individuals to work more than 12 hours a day, six days a week, with restricted toilet break times and no meal breaks.

Stories such as Foxconn's tend to capture public attention for a certain amount of time, and hopes are raised that the underlying issues will be addressed, so that no more similar incidents take place in the future. New scandals of this type, however, are reported on a regular basis, indicating that the fundamental issues are yet to be resolved, and that employment in global supply chains remains a problematic aspect of IB. Traditionally, particularly in the western world, the governance of employment was a responsibility of the state and was exercised through legislation regarding, for example: minimum wages for workers, enforcement of contractual obligations, dismissal procedures and the recognition of trade unions. In addition, workers were able to influence the conditions of their employment through a process of collective bargaining with the employers (Traxler, 1999). Now, working conditions across much of the world are not regulated through national or international governance mechanisms. In many countries, government control over employment conditions has decreased as a result of privatization and deregulation. Outside of Western Europe, trade unionism and collective bargaining cultures are weak or even non-existent. Through a two-way 'social dumping' mechanism operating in contemporary IB, firms move from countries with high labour standards to cheaper production locations. At the same time, governments are often reluctant to implement labour protection laws that might reduce their nation's 'competitiveness' and 'attractiveness' in the eyes of MNCs (Donaghey and Teague, 2006).

In recent years there has been growing pressure on MNCs to address poor working conditions in global supply chain factories through adopting private, sometimes also referred to as 'soft', regulatory initiatives (Knudsen, 2013). This pressure has come from stakeholders such as NGOs, consumer organizations, trade unions and the media, campaigning for regulation of business practices in global supply chains (Büthe, 2010). An example of a private, business-driven initiative aimed at improving working conditions in the factories and farms across the world is the Business for Social Compliance Initiative (BSCI), established in 2003 by a group of large European retailers as a vehicle for monitoring and auditing the social performance of their suppliers globally using a uniform set of standards and audit criteria (Egels-Zandén and WahlQvist, 2007). The BSCI declares as its vision 'a world of free trade and sustainable global supply chains, in which factories and farms are compliant with national labour legislation as well as with ILO Conventions protecting workers' rights' (BSCI, 2016). The organization offers one common Code of Conduct and one Implementation System covering a range of global supply chain labour issues applicable to companies producing all kinds of products in any location across the world.

The BSCI Code of Conduct draws on international labour standards such as those included in the conventions and declarations of the International Labour Organization (ILO), the United Nations' (UN) Guiding Principles on Business and Human Rights, and the Organization for Economic Cooperation and Development's (OECD) guidelines for MNCs. The Code sets out 11 core labour rights that are supposed to be gradually implemented by organizations subscribing to BSCI and their business partners. These 11 rights include: freedom of association and collective bargaining; fair remuneration; occupational health and safety; special protection for young workers; no bonded labour; ethical business behavior; no discrimination; decent working hours; no child labour; no precarious employment; and protection of the environment. The companies that are signatories to the BSCI Code must observe its social and environmental standards. Those companies that are also suppliers are responsible for making sure that the Code is observed by their sub-contractors. Placing responsibility on companies to impose the rules of the Code on their sub-contractors acknowledges that actors within global supply chains do not have equal power. Some, usually large MNCs, are referred to as 'lead firms' and exert more power in the chain than others. One effect of this power imbalance can be a pressure on sub-contractors by lead firms to reduce prices. On the other hand, it can also manifest itself in demands to improve conditions for the workers even where this is not demanded by state laws. Threatened by the prospect of losing their contract with the MNC, sub-contractors are likely to submit to this kind of pressure and, consequently, improve the working conditions for those they employ.

Critics of business-driven initiatives such as the BSCI have highlighted that the task of safeguarding employment conditions in global supply chains should not be left to businesses themselves. As an alternative, multi-stakeholder initiatives with aims similar to those of the BSCI have been established. An example of this is the Ethical Trading Initiative (ETI): an association of trade unions, NGOs and company members from different industries and countries of origin including the UK as well as Australia, Germany, Spain, Sweden and the USA. It has been recognized that ETI's Base Code of Labour Practice is stricter and has more control mechanisms than BSCI's Code of Conduct (Fransen and Burgoon, 2012). However, it has also been acknowledged that both business- and multi-stakeholder-driven regulatory initiatives have significant shortcomings. As research suggests, codes of conduct do not necessarily lead to improvements in corporate social and environmental performance (Bondy et al., 2008). Moreover, even in the case of multi-stakeholder initiatives such as ETI, MNCs tend to play the role of the most powerful and influential stakeholder, and one that has the greatest control over the standards and mechanisms developed by the members (Donaghey et al., 2014).

Linking consumers and supply chains in IB

As our earlier examples relating to the impact of consumers on IB practice illustrate, for global supply chain employment conditions to see a marked improvement, it might be necessary for customers to assume an active role in shaping the governance of labour standards (cf. Riisgaard and Hammer, 2011). In the past, consumers were viewed as either irrelevant to producers' working conditions or even as a source of an additional 'burden' on workers, for example through placing demands regarding flexibility and service quality (Kessler and Bach, 2011). At present, consumers have come to be seen as 'a fundamental post-production actor and driver of labor governance rather than an enemy of labor as a result of labor standards' (Donaghey et al., 2014: 233). It is recognized that many customers are able and willing to make purchase decisions on the basis of, among other factors, the conditions in which products are manufactured and services are delivered. This creates a potentially strong link between geographically dispersed and highly diverse stakeholder categories in contemporary IB – consumers and producers – to the point of being able to counter-balance the centrality and extent of power exercised by MNCs. For instance, MNCs are not legally responsible for the breaches in human rights that might occur on the premises of their independent suppliers. As a result of consumer pressure, however, it is now widely expected that no human rights abuses should take place at any production stages preceding the delivery of final products to customers (Bartley, 2007). Further, it has been argued that these days, actions directed by customers in rich industrialized countries at producers who are associated with unethical business practices go beyond boycotting goods marketed by those producers, as in the example of Fruit of the Loom discussed above. In addition to boycotting 'unwanted' products and firms, consumers are considered inclined to deliberately choose products with explicitly positive ethical connotations (Schmelzer, 2010), such as those bearing a Fairtrade certification.

At this point, however, it needs to be added that the relationship between consumers' actions and MNCs' practices is more complex and cannot be reduced to a direct causal relationship between customers' purchase decisions and changes in the working conditions across global supply chains. The primary way in which 'consumers' voice' influences businesses is through the efforts of activists and NGOs. It has also been pointed out that there is a limit to the extent consumer power can replace a legal framework in ensuring decent working conditions in global supply chains. After all, not all consumers enjoy the level of income that allows them to base their purchasing decisions on ethical, rather than purely economic, grounds. Those who face affordability issues, in particular, might not be keen to purchase ethically produced goods as these are usually also more expensive. Similarly, not all MNCs whose supply chains are characterized by ethically dubious practices market products to individual customers. Those that do not have a recognizable brand that is attractive to relatively high-income consumers in western countries are likely to escape potential consumer pressure. These caveats notwithstanding, it is necessary to realize that as a consequence of globalization, different stakeholders in IB have become more strongly connected, and especially consumers have gained a greater role in setting standards and improving labour conditions in global supply chains.

Impact of IB on communities and society

Poverty and inequality remain big issues in the contemporary world. In the context of understanding the impact of IB on communities and society at large in an economic sense, it is important to explore the ways in which international businesses currently influence – and potentially how they could influence – economic development. Here, we would like to draw your attention to the conceptualization of economic growth postulated by the Nobel Laureate Amartya Sen (1983, 1999). According to Sen, we should not view the notion of economic development purely in terms of traditional economic indicators such as aggregate income or gross domestic product generated by the population. Rather, we should include in our definition an improvement in the capabilities, entitlements and – importantly – freedoms of members of society. The expansion of freedom is understood as both the main means and key outcome of development. Sen (1999) distinguishes between five interconnected freedoms that should progress along with the economic development process: political freedoms, economic facilities, social opportunities, transparency guarantees and protective security.

Applying Sen's (1999) understanding of economic development in practice would mean aiming at the accomplishment of a state where MNCs relate to all stakeholders in a way that results in not disadvantaging or exploiting any stakeholder groups. Ultimately, this would also bring about reduction in global poverty and inequalities. The reality of global economy and stakeholder relations in IB, however, is currently far from such a state. Its achievement would require a significant change in how the needs and interests of different groups affected by IB are treated by companies. For MNCs to be able to relate to all stakeholders in line with Sen's (1999) five freedoms requires that firms' managers 'put themselves in the stakeholder's place and try to empathize with that stakeholder's position' (Freeman et al., 2007: 112). Adopting a stakeholder-based perspective on IB operations and effects has been advocated in several streams of academic literature. This way of thinking has also had influence on the practices of MNCs towards communities and society in general. An example of this lies in 'triple bottom line' (TBL) accounting (Elkington, 1998), where a firm's performance is evaluated through a three-way focus on its economic, environmental and social wellbeing-related impacts. Adopting TBL, it is now common practice amongst companies, and in particular MNCs, to prepare and make publicly available not only their financial but also their environmental and social reports. It has also been acknowledged that TBL has brought to the mainstream an emphasis on a longer-term view that moves away from a preoccupation with short-term profit maximization of and return on investment. However, environmental and social reporting has also been criticized as constituting little more than a public relations tool that aims at glossing over the possible negative impacts of a firm on its stakeholders.

The above discussion demonstrates that caution needs to be exercised when both possible positive and negative contributions of companies, especially MNCs, to the achievement of societal goals, are evaluated. As Banerjee (2014) points out, the dynamics of the influence of business on society are not only shaped by businesses but also by factors belonging to the broader institutional and legal environment. Whether IB companies exert a positive or negative impact on communities and society at large will depend, for example, on the role of governments and other governance structures enabling and shaping the activities of MNCs in particular ways. Below we present two examples – one positive and one problematic – of the effects of IB on local communities, and demonstrate how these illustrate the complex dynamics between businesses and other important players.

A positive impact of corporate-driven initiatives on communities is often cited in the case of the Bill and Melinda Gates Foundation whose aim is to 'help all people lead healthy, productive lives' (Gates Foundation, 2016). The Foundation's activities are organized under four programme areas: Global Development Division, Global Health Division, The United States Division, and Global Policy and Advocacy. In 2015, the Foundation allocated $4.2 billion in grants. One of the initiatives that the Foundation supports is the charity Save the Children's Saving Newborn Lives (SNL) Programme. Currently, the Programme focuses on seven priority countries. In four of these – Bangladesh, Malawi, Nepal and Uganda – substantial policy and systemic changes have already been achieved. Here, SNL now 'works through partnerships with government and stakeholders to achieve and document the scale-up of newborn health interventions' (Save the Children, 2016a). In the remaining three – Ethiopia, India and Nigeria – the Programme 'provides direct support to the design, development and implementation of national strategies and policies to improve the quality and availability of care for mothers and newborns' (ibid.). Thanks to the work of SNL, the availability of and access to both routine and emergency newborn services have improved, and demand for newborn care has increased. As a result of this and similar initiatives, the number of newborn deaths across the world has reduced from 5.1 million in 1990 to 2.7 million in 2015 (Save the Children, 2016b). The example of the Gates Foundation shows the possibilities for re-directing funding from MNCs' profits to benefit local communities and bring about positive social outcomes. At the same time, it demonstrates how achieving these requires joint work on the part of multiple stakeholders, including governments, NGOs and businesses.

Similarly, where MNCs' impacts on local communities and society are reported to be problematic, the actions of a number of stakeholders need to be taken into account to understand how outcomes emerge. It is not sufficient to only look at the actions of businesses, but is also necessary to analyse the role of national governments and other authorities in creating and maintaining conditions in which companies' influence on local populations can be negative. The example of the palm oil industry in Sri Lanka presents a case in point. Since the 1990s, Sri Lanka's governments have gradually been handing over the country's land from indigenous communities to private companies (Johnson, 2015). These companies have been using the land primarily to plant fast-growing timber species used in the production of pulp and paper, as well as palm oil. Palm oil expansion has caused deforestation of the country, whereas the presence of businesses growing palm oil has resulted in numerous conflicts between the businesses and the local communities. Sirait (2009) has conducted research into the conflict between palm oil companies and the indigenous people of the Sri Lankan region of West Kalimantan. His findings suggest that the oil plantations have been beneficial to very few members of local populations, namely the local elite. For the vast majority of West Kalimantan indigenous people, the plantations have resulted in them being deprived of land and forced to pursue livelihoods based on activities other than farming. These often involve migration either on a temporary or permanent basis. Women and marginalized members of indigenous communities have been the most disadvantaged groups with regard to diminished livelihood options. The changes in ways of securing livelihoods have, in turn, had social and cultural impacts, whereby members of the communities are no longer able to observe their customs connected to living and cultivating ancestral land. Formerly collectively-owned descendant group lands and household lands have become individualized. In the process, this has damaged solidarity amongst the local people, creating conflicts between families and individuals.

While on the surface, it might seem that IB companies are the main culprit behind the multiple negative effects of the palm oil industry in Sri Lanka, the role of other stakeholders – in particular the national government and local authorities – should not be overlooked. To start with, the underlying conditions for deforestation and conflict have been created by the Sri Lankan government allowing land to be taken over for palm oil plantation purposes. Local authorities, on the other hand, have been guilty of corruption in relation to allocating land. Local corruption problems, in turn, have not been addressed by the central government whose responsibility it has been to ensure transparency and law enforcement regarding land allocation in the country.

Conclusion

In this chapter we discussed how organizations in IB affect and are affected by people – specifically, different stakeholders. We also demonstrated some of the complexity and dynamics characterizing stakeholder relations in IB. Arguably, firms, especially MNCs, are the most powerful actor in IB environment, influencing in different ways the lives of their employees and managers, consumers and suppliers, local communities and society at large. At the same time, MNCs' activities are influenced by each of these parties. Further, one stakeholder group's actions directed at businesses can affect the situation of another stakeholder group, often located at a considerable geographical distance.

Both positive and negative outcomes of IB activity result from a number of factors and decisions, some of which are beyond the control of companies. We encourage you to think of the complexity and multi-directionality of relations in IB. We also propose that when you think about stakeholders, in the first place you think 'people'. Understanding that every stakeholder category – businesses, employees, suppliers, NGOs, governments, local communities, society – consists of individuals who have interests, desires and stakes in what is happening in the world, allows us to see all these categories of stakeholders in a less abstract, less distant and a more personal way. This, in turn, has the capacity to inspire us to think of what changes are needed within the current model of IB to make sure that the pursuit of one group's interests does not involve compromising the interests of another party, and that ultimately IB serves to improve the lives of people, both now and in the future.

Questions

1. As international aid budgets decline, corporate philanthropy is seen by some as holding a promise for fostering international development. Critics, however, question the motivations behind 'corporate giving' as well as the extent to which private foundations influence policy-making in areas such as public health and education. Using examples, discuss the pros and cons of corporate philanthropy from the perspective of corporations and societies in both developed and developing countries.
2. Reflecting on your answer to Q1, what governance solutions would you propose at a global level to address issues of poverty and inequality between and within societies?
3. Consumer activism in combination with industry codes of conduct are often considered the main means for improving working conditions in global supply chains. Who, in your view, should bear responsibility for these issues, and what accountability mechanisms are required in order for this responsibility to be carried out effectively?

Further reading

Aluchna, M. and Idowu, S.O. (2016) (eds) *The Dynamics of Corporate Social Responsibility: A Critical Approach to Theory and Practice.* New York: Springer.

Bartley, T., Koos, S., Samel, H., Setrini, G. and Summers, N. (2015) *Looking Behind the Label. Global Industries and the Conscientious Consumer*. Bloomington, IN: Indiana University Press.

War on Want (2013) *The Living Wage. Winning the Fight for Social Justice*. Available at: http://media.waronwant.org/sites/default/files/The%20Living%20Wage%20-%20War%20on%20Want.PDF?_ga=1.12055092.1698148290.1471495684 (accessed 21 September 2016).

7

Understanding Organizations in the IB Environment

Introduction

Based on the theoretical approaches and examples we have outlined in earlier chapters, you should now be able to understand why organizations might operate as they do, and why different types of organizations do different things in different ways. We have introduced critical approaches and have discussed examples of IB practice, including those at the margins of legality and morality. We have done this to prompt your thinking on the full range of impacts of contemporary organizations in and on the world at large. Specifically, in Chapter 6, we discussed the complex nature of relations between IB firms and their multiple stakeholders.

In this chapter, we introduce you to some analytic methods that will enable you to develop your own understanding and to conduct a critical inquiry into the impact that organizations you choose to study or work with have, or might have on the full range of stakeholders, both now and in future. In clarifying who are stakeholders, we return to the work of Ed Freeman, who defines them as, '(a)ny identifiable group or individual who can affect the achievement of an organization's objectives' (Freeman and Reed, 1983: 91). More importantly, they are 'individuals, human beings ... moral beings' (Freeman, 1994: 411). In discussing stakeholders, much of the IB literature focuses attention on those – more usually organizations than individuals – with direct financial or business links to the IB firm. These include financial shareholders/stockholders, suppliers and customers. In contrast, we advocate a more inclusive approach that addresses stakeholders as individual human beings.

In the rest of this chapter, we present a number of critical methods for opening up discussion of impacts in the broader environment. First, we introduce stakeholder analysis to prompt more detailed consideration of groups and individuals that can both affect and be affected by organizations' decisions and actions. Here, we encourage a particular focus on identifying those who are more remote and often excluded from consideration. Second, we outline a structured approach for exploring the broad IB environment. PESTEL analysis directs your consideration to the full range of the interconnected factors – political, economic, social, technological and legal – that have current and potential future impacts on a particular IB issue. Third, building on the first two, we outline a taxonomy, or framework, for investigating issues of ethics and legality in relation to forms of IB. We highlight that these two areas are not necessarily dependent on each other. Fourth, we expand our discussion of the contemporary relevance of Aristotle's intellectual virtue of *phronēsis*. We again draw on its interpretation in Flyvbjerg's (2001) set of value-rational questions. You will see that it is embedded in the various approaches in this chapter. Finally, we introduce you to the use of scenario methods, in particular 'critical scenario method' (CSM) (Cairns et al., 2010; Wright and Cairns, 2011). Scenario analysis provides a structured approach for exploring different ways that the future might unfold over the next five to ten years. CSM combines basic scenario method using PESTEL analysis with both stakeholder analysis and the application of *phronēsis*. The key aim of CSM is to explore the implications of different possible futures for all involved and affected stakeholders, in particular those that are powerless but clearly impacted.

Understanding the full range of stakeholders

In Chapter 6 we outlined the difference between an organization's stakeholders and narrower and more exclusive groups such as shareholders/stockholders and customers. We also drew attention to the importance of considering relationships of power among the broad stakeholder constituency. Here, we introduce a basic model of stakeholder analysis to encourage you to think not only about who the stakeholders are in relation to any IB issue but also on their relative power. We prompt you to consider the varying levels of interest that different individuals and groups may have in the issue at different points in time, and what this means for others. We highlight that a stakeholder that has a high degree of power to influence any situation may not necessarily be interested in the issue at a point in time. In this case, they may be unlikely to exercise their power without some form of prompting. This form of stakeholder analysis can be undertaken in accordance with Figure 7.1 opposite.

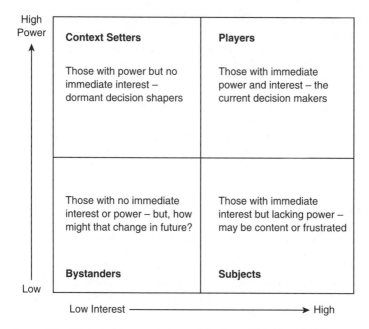

High Power		
Context Setters	**Players**	
Those with power but no immediate interest – dormant decision shapers	Those with immediate power and interest – the current decision makers	
Those with no immediate interest or power – but, how might that change in future?	Those with immediate interest but lacking power – may be content or frustrated	
Bystanders	**Subjects**	

Low Interest ⟶ High

Figure 7.1 Stakeholder analysis matrix (from Wright and Cairns, 2011; reproduced with permission of Palgrave Macmillan)

The stakeholders that have an immediate interest in the issue under consideration and a high degree of power to influence it are called 'players'. This category will likely include senior operational management of the MNC, key customers or clients and others directly involved in how the issue is currently unfolding. However, the second type, called 'context setters' are central to analysis of the situation. This group may include very powerful parties, such as politicians, institutional shareholders, senior executive management and even bodies like international NGOs and media companies. It is very easy to think that because they have power they will have interest in exercising it. However, if the issue is not sufficiently high up the agenda of such busy groups and individuals, they may have little or no awareness of it. But, if something should happen that awakens their interest, particularly some negative event, they may suddenly take notice and bring their power to bear on what happens next.

The third group is called the 'subjects'. These stakeholders have a high degree of interest in the issue, but lack power to influence it. These may include home nation employees of the MNC, individual customers and small suppliers. However, the group may include remote and largely ignored host country workers for sub-contractors operating under sweatshop conditions, or future generations whose land is being exploited and polluted for present gain. The final group are categorized as 'bystanders', with no current interest or power. But, as Figure 7.1 points out, this situation may change in future.

If you analyse the current status of an issue in IB that interests you, the use of this matrix can give you a clearer picture of who all the involved and affected parties are. It can guide your thinking on who is directly involved and is driving the issue forward now. It also prompts you to consider those that may be directly affected but that have no influence on the outcome. Additionally, it will enable you to identify powerful stakeholders that might be able to impact the issue, but who are not currently doing so, and why this might be the case.

As the above outline suggests, stakeholder relationships are not static. Rather, they are complex and dynamic and, as such, positions can move in future. Some powerful parties can bring about change themselves, while others will be located in the matrix according to actions and events beyond their control. All stakeholders' positions can be changed by external impacting events that affect the nature of the issue under consideration. We develop this line of discussion below.

The organization and its environment – PESTEL and SWOT analyses

Two of the most commonly used models for undertaking a basic analysis of an organization's business environment are PEST (and its derivatives PESTEL, STEEPL and other similar acronyms) and SWOT analyses. The acronym PEST refers to the political, economic, social and technological factors that are impacting or will impact the organization. These should be considered at all levels relevant to the particular organization and its environment. For example, the political environment will be impacted by global and supranational events, such as US Presidential elections, policymaking within the EU, and relations between nations such as Brazil, China and India and their neighbours. It will also be defined by national and local political events and activities including, as relevant: state, regional and local elections; local government policies and practices; activity by NGOs and direct-action groups; and the actions of concerned individuals in the affected community. Similarly, technological factors may be hi- or lo-tech, but must be relevant to the issue and to the particular stakeholders under consideration. Examples might range from the nature of Internet connectivity to the availability of reliable local water or electricity supplies. The basic PEST model has been expanded to take account, first, of legal factors (PESTL), again including international, national and local legislative frameworks as appropriate. More recently, ecological or environment factors have been integrated into the framework (PESTEL), to consider global, national and local impacts relevant to the issue under consideration.

PESTEL analysis can usefully be implemented in conjunction with stakeholder analysis when exploring some complex, ambiguous and dynamic IB problems. Considering the political factors that will influence and drive the issue in the future, it is important to identify who the political stakeholders are. You can analyse their current and potential future status of power over the issue, their level of interest in exerting this power under different circumstances, and the possible outcomes – positive and negative – that might arise from exercise of power. Similarly, to understand the nature of technological factors that will influence the issue, it is crucial to know who the technology players and context setters are and, again, to consider their relations of interest in and power over the issue. As with any framework that aims at structuring and categorizing complex problems with a view to subjecting them to rational analysis, we caution you against a mechanistic application of PESTEL. Our intent is to present PESTEL as a possible set of prompts to open up a comprehensive appraisal of interconnected and dynamic issues, and to avoid myopic, single discipline-focused approaches. To further guide your thinking on structured analysis of the future possibilities we refer to here, we introduce scenario analysis later in this chapter.

While the PEST-based models facilitate an inclusive approach to exploring the external environment in which the organization operates, SWOT analysis looks more closely at how it stands up within that context. First, it prompts an appraisal of what are the organization's core strengths (S) and what are its critical weaknesses (W) for thriving or surviving. These are assessed in relation to identified opportunities (O) and threats (T) in the external environment, as explored through the PESTEL framework. We would point out that SWOT analysis has been critiqued as being reductionist and simplistic. Some factors might represent either a strength or a weakness. For example, being the best and most specialized producer of 'widgets' might be a great strength if the market and demand for widgets is strong. However, if this market collapses and there are no prospective customers, such specialization with no diversity can become a severe weakness. Further, what one category of stakeholders might consider to be strengths and/or opportunities, others might see as weaknesses and/or threats. For example, weak employment protections in an LDC would likely be viewed as an opportunity by the MNC's shareholders. However, for an NGO tackling poverty in the country it would represent a threat. If its limitations are recognized and acknowledged, the application of a SWOT analysis can enhance your understanding of a complex IB problem and inspire your thinking on what is possible and what is desirable for the IB organization and its stakeholders.

A taxonomy of IB legality and ethics

Having introduced models for considering stakeholders and their status, the IB environment and its dynamics, and the potential for action by the IB organization within these contexts, we now introduce a critical assessment of issues of legality and ethics/morality in relation to courses of action. As-Saber and Cairns (2015) provide a taxonomy for considering where any IB activity sits, first, in terms of formal legal structures. These include both international and different national legislatures. Second, it prompts thinking in terms of the ethical/moral status of the activity, recognizing that matters of legality and of ethics and morality need not be linked to each other. The fact that an IB activity is legal does not mean that it is necessarily ethical, and that it may be considered unethical by some does not mean that it is seen as immoral and unethical by all. Similarly, what is legal within one jurisdiction may be illegal within another. Undertaking IB activity across multiple legal and ethical contexts requires that you must be aware of these differences.

For As-Saber and Cairns, questions of ethics are not set within a universal framework that is absolute and applicable in relation to each and every activity. Rather, as for the legal frameworks, ethics are considered to be dependent on context. They must be guided by the social and moral norms of the parties whose interests are being considered. As such, consideration of ethics here is linked to Aristotle's *phronēsis* and Flyvbjerg's (2001) analytic framework that we discuss below. Aristotle's virtue of *phronēsis* – or 'practical wisdom' to inform action for the good of society – forms the thread that connects this section, those preceding, and the models that follow. Together, they offer a comprehensive approach to exploring IB activities in terms of their broad impacts, rather than merely their profitability or marketability. The outline of As-Saber and Cairns' (2015) taxonomy, and the key questions that it inspires, is shown in Figure 7.2.

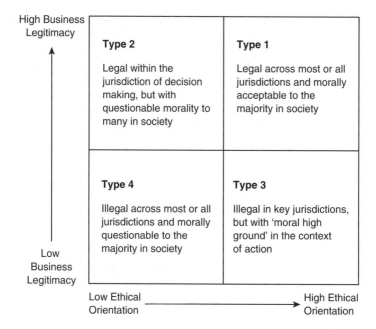

Figure 7.2   A taxonomy of 'Black international business' (based upon As-Saber and Cairns, 2015; reproduced with permission of Routledge, Taylor & Francis Group)

The vertical axis of 'business legitimacy' refers to questions of legality and illegality. While these may seem fairly straightforward, IB activity can be subject to a diverse range of legislative frameworks that may not be consistent. These include the tenets of international law and those of the various nations across which the activity is spread – from raw material sources, through manufacturing locations, to sales and service centres and customer bases. Activities that are perfectly legal in one country may be illegal in another, causing issues even for the firm that is focused on being legitimate in all its activities. Of greater concern, however, are situations in which organizations and individuals break, bend or ignore relevant legal frameworks, both national and international. In recent years, issues of legality have been raised in relation to numerous cases. Many relate to activities in the so-called less-developed countries. However, others are centred in advanced economies, ranging from questions on the legality of child labour in American tobacco plantations (cf. Becker, 2014) to those of illegal consumer downloads in Australia (cf. Davidson, 2015).

While issues of legality may be unclear, there will generally be a legislative framework – or set of frameworks – that can and should be referred to for clarification. However, questions of the ethics and morality of IB activities have no such foundations to fall back on across many contexts. Granted, there are nations in which both legal and moral frameworks are interrelated, such as those where both law and ethics are informed by the Quran. The personal ethical framework of many people will be influenced by other religious beliefs, but in countries where these are individual values rather than being legally binding, ethical questions frequently become matters of personal choice; for example, whether or not to drink alcohol, to smoke tobacco or to consume animal products. Issues raised in Chapter 6, such as selling to the poor and the marketing of race, can also be seen as matters of individual choice, but we view them as grounds for broader and more critical debate. In the field of IB, questions of ethics might be asked in relation to some of the biggest trade relations in the world, such as the sales of armaments to countries that use them against segments of their own population, or the extraction of minerals from land that is held to be of spiritual significance by its traditional owners.

The taxonomy is readily completed for activities that fall clearly and unequivocally into either Type 1 or Type 4 – being considered either both legal and moral across all contexts, or both illegal and unethical across all. However, matters become more complex when an activity is seen by substantial numbers of stakeholders as lying within either Type 2 or Type 3. While we might assume that executives of involved MNCs consider their activities as both legal and ethical, to others, forms of trade such as those mentioned above – armaments, tobacco, alcohol – would be classed as Type 2. Here, they are acknowledged to be legal but are viewed as being morally questionable. Type 3 activities are less numerous and more difficult to identify. However, As-Saber and Cairns (2015) refer to the example where South Africa supported the moral case for development and manufacture of pharmaceuticals to treat HIV and AIDS, in breach of international patents and the laws of multinational pharmaceutical businesses' home nations. This was a complex case where, over time, the MNCs first sought to sue the South African government and then withdrew their case, the government subsequently enacted laws to enable local production of drugs in partnership with the MNCs, and the medical NGO *Médecins Sans Frontières* (MSF) later defied these laws to import cheaper generic drugs from Brazil (cf. Schoofs, 2002).

We see this taxonomy of legal and ethical consideration as enabling you to gain a deeper understanding of the complex nature of IB. It can help you to comprehend why some activities provoke very different responses across nations and between stakeholders. Also, we hope that it will be of value to you in terms of both making personal choices about your own activities and of understanding why others may see the world and behave differently.

From analysis to action – phronetic inquiry

To this point, we have outlined a few frameworks and models for exploring and understanding how IB activities operate in the present time, for undertaking your own case study analysis. Now, we move on to consider several modes of inquiry that are designed not only to explore what is happening, but to elicit ideas on how things might be done differently, for what reasons, and with what impacts – both socially and ecologically, and both now and in the future. First, we return to Bent Flyvbjerg's (2001) value-rational question framework based on Aristotle's intellectual virtue, *phronēsis*. As we state above, this virtue is directed at moral/ethical deliberation in order to inform action for the good of humanity. It deals with matters of context and with individual beliefs and values that guide what is considered 'good'. Flyvbjerg's contemporary interpretation of Aristotle leads him to present four questions to guide this thinking. These are:

1. Where are we going?
2. Is this desirable?
3. What, if anything, should we do about it?

Finally, recognizing that the path from thinking to action requires engagement with issues of power – or lack of it – Flyvbjerg's fourth question is:

4. Who gains and who loses, and by which mechanisms of power?

These seemingly simple questions require us to think critically and deeply about the realities of where we *are* going. Are we heading in a direction that will lead to a state of good for humanity and the environment? Or, are we extracting and exploiting for short-term profit and gain for the few, while leaving a legacy of decay and desolation for the many and for future generations? The second question leads directly into honest appraisal of these issues, particularly when the notion of what is 'desirable' is subject to critical inquiry. Again, we have to think broadly on for whom any particular activity is desirable and for what reasons, and for whom it is likely to be highly undesirable, due to exclusion from any benefit or exposure to any loss and damage. The third question brings us to personal deliberation about what course of action *we* might choose to take. Building on the concepts that underpin As-Saber and Cairns' taxonomy, we can first consider if action is required in order to remain, or return to being within the law. Then, we can contemplate the moral/ethical implications of what is currently being done.

Recognizing what can, should or will be done about something involves choices that will not necessarily be desirable to all. Flyvbjerg's final question brings into the open issues of who are the winners and losers from any particular course of action. Answering it requires explicit acknowledgement of the means by which power was exerted to bring about a specific outcome. Was this based upon legitimate and legal authority, whether or not it may be ethically questionable? Or, was it based on some illicit exercise of power, whether through open threat, surreptitious coercion or bribery and corruption? Did it bring about a better outcome for the majority of affected stakeholders? Or, did it benefit the few and reinforce current socio-economic fragmentation?

Here, we bring your attention back to the stakeholder matrix, and consideration of which stakeholders hold both power over and interest in any IB issue at a point in time. Which hold power but appear to be lacking interest at present? Which have a high degree of interest but lack power to bring about change? Are there powerful context setters whose interest, if it is awakened, may align with the interests of the powerless subjects? If so, by what form of political or social engagement might these parties be brought together? If this happens, what might be the results of their interaction?

The taxonomy of legality and ethics enables us to understand what is happening in a particular sphere of IB activity from a static perspective. In contrast, phronetic inquiry requires both that we contemplate alternative courses of action in response to what is currently happening and that we explicitly address issues of power that might be surfaced from stakeholder analysis. In the next section, we move on to provide a structured framework for consideration of the most complex and ambiguous of questions – what might the future hold in store? We do this by introducing scenario analysis. Unlike some models for exploring the future – such as probability analysis or forecasting, that seek to provide *the* answer to what the future *will* be – scenario methods are designed to explore the 'limits of possibility and plausibility' for what *might* happen.

Critical scenario method (CSM)

In recent decades, 'scenario planning' has become widely used by organizations, both governments and businesses, particularly since the events of 11 September 2001. Organizations use scenarios to consider, first, how the future might unfold in a range of ways, and second, how their current strategies perform against different futures. Governments, including Singapore, have used scenarios to explore the potential impacts of issues like climate change, new technologies and demographic shifts. Scenario methods (e.g. Wright and Cairns, 2011) outline structured approaches to construction of a range of possible and plausible futures within which organizations may find themselves operating. They consider how the future is both uncertain and unpredictable, but is also to a degree knowable and understandable. They facilitate thinking on how the organization has options as to what actions it may initiate, and that different courses of action will have different impacts and outcomes. Wright and Cairns (2011) outline what they term the 'basic method' of scenario generation based on a structured analysis of present data, facts and informed opinions projected forward to a horizon year appropriate to the problem – normally about five to ten years ahead.

We do not have space here to cover the whole of the basic method, but the fundamental stages include:

1. First, a clear and concise statement of the problem to be explored, agreed by all.
2. PESTEL analysis to identify 'driving forces' – clearly defined political, economic, etc. issues that will determine how the problem situation will evolve, normally generating a very substantial list of driving forces.
3. 'Clustering' the driving forces to identify a smaller number of broader factors that take account of cause/effect and chronological links between driving forces.
4. Defining two extreme outcomes for conditions that might prevail as a result of the unfolding of each factor – in simple terms, 'best' and 'worst' cases.
5. Determining which two factors will have the highest impact on the problem, but with a high degree of uncertainty as to what that impact might be – best or worst?
6. Outlining general descriptions of the world under four sets of conditions for these uncertain outcomes of two factors: best/best, best/worst, worst/best, worst/worst.

7. Writing up scenario narratives that tell believable stories of these futures, and of the events and actors that have led to things being as they are as each unfolds.

These scenarios tell of four different possible and plausible futures arising from the same conditions in the present. They do so as a result of the variety of choices, decisions and events that might occur over their timescale. These might include: political choices and elections; business decisions and actions; economic prosperity or stagnation; social stability or unrest; technological breakthroughs or failures; ecological protection or environmental degradation; and strong legal protections or criminality and abuse. They will consider both global and national as well as regional and local possibilities. Drawing on human capacity for 'intuitive logic' to write believable scenario narratives, you will see that certain links of causality and chronology make sense while others are patently absurd. These will include interconnections within and between PESTEL factors. For example, the technological infrastructure available to the electorate will influence who is going to cast a vote, and thereby the outcome of political elections. None of the scenarios is a 'prediction' of the future. As such, they are individually meaningless. The four only work as a set, to delineate the boundaries within which the future is likely to unfold. Hence, the world remains unpredictable, but becomes more knowable.

In designing strategies to respond to scenarios, MNCs may make choices in terms of purely financial criteria – seeking shareholder/stockholder value and returns. However, we focus on approaches for assessing other, social and environmental, targets and outcomes. Specifically, recognizing the full range of IB activities and organizations that we have discussed in this book – from the clearly criminal to the highly legal but morally questionable – we work with 'critical scenario method' (CSM) (Cairns et al., 2010; Wright and Cairns, 2011). CSM surfaces issues of legality and morality in IB decision making and action. It embeds Flyvbjerg's (2001) interpretation of Aristotelian *phronēsis* and his value-rational question framework in order to prompt critical inquiry.

In CSM, a set of four scenarios is developed in line with the basic method. However, it requires a stakeholder analysis to identify the full range of involved and affected stakeholders, including those remote and excluded. Each of the four scenarios sets out a different answer to Flyvbjerg's first question – where are we going? These prompt us to think about the second question – is this desirable? – in different ways, in relation to all stakeholders. What is desirable to one party in one scenario may be undesirable to another, while the reverse may be the case under conditions of another of the scenarios. Here, we consider the different scenarios in terms of legality and ethics and from the perspectives of different stakeholders. Thinking on the third question – what if anything should we do? – forces us to evaluate our own position within the world and in relation to the issue at hand. Finally, Flyvbjerg's fourth question requires explicit appraisal of our stakeholder analysis and the status of power over and interest in the problem across the four scenarios. We must assess the potential impacts of different courses of action by powerful stakeholders on others.

Remembering that Aristotle's *phronēsis* defines a form of thinking to inform action, to avoid worst case scenario conditions for humanity in general we must question how alternative power structures might be established and activated. We can consider the potential power of individuals and groups to bring about change: the media, consumer bodies, pressure groups, etc. As we illustrate below, there are historical examples of how alternative social structures have been built to mobilize new forms of power and to trigger transformation for a general good. However, there are also examples of how misdirected and malevolent forms of power and interest have prevailed, despite potential scenario pointers to the contrary, to the detriment of the many and the benefit of a privileged few.

While we can only give a broad overview of CSM here and refer you to other work for more detailed coverage of its full implementation, the principles that underpin it are straightforward and worthy of summary, as follows:

1. For any complex, ambiguous and wicked problem, do not try to predict the future.
2. Instead, consider the PESTEL factors that will drive it and the range of possible outcomes.
3. Think carefully about all the involved and affected stakeholders.
4. Who stands to gain and who to lose if we continue as we are going?
5. Is there a better way forward?
6. What can I do and what am I going to do to try to make the future better?

Consider the following example of the type of complex decision that might be examined by management of an MNC in this way. A firm has a manufacturing unit in a high-cost economy, but one that is profitable. The company is the only major employer in the city and a number of small local firms are reliant upon it as suppliers. However, the firm has established a new plant in a low-cost economy that is achieving the necessary quality standards and generating higher profits by a factor of three. This plant is situated in an export processing zone (EPZ) along with a large number of major MNCs. Workers must be brought in from other parts of the country and live in dormitory blocks. Reflect on some of the questions facing the MNC's management under shareholder pressure to relocate all manufacturing to the low-cost economy. Does shareholder return take precedence, legally and ethically? What are the short- and long-term implications of alternatives? How do shareholder and stakeholder interests vary? This example can be used to 'test' our individual values by simple consideration of Flyvbjerg's questions.

Scenario analysis – examples of potential and failure

Statements of the positive impact of scenario analysis can be found in numerous forms. An example of this is the centrality of scenario thinking to the transition of South Africa in the 1990s and the release of Nelson Mandela (Kahane, 2007). However, we can also point to high profile and high impact events that have unfolded with no apparent consideration of possibility and plausibility in advance, despite early warning indicators in the broad environment.

First, one of us was a regular visitor to Hong Kong in the 1990s, teaching MBA students for a number of years that included both before and after the 'handback' of Hong Kong from British to Chinese government administration. This was an event that had been programmed into history to some extent for almost a century – the period of Britain's lease on the New Territories. As China refused to extend the lease, handback of the entire Hong Kong territory was pretty much unavoidable, due to the geographical, infrastructural and economic ties that bound it together. With the complexity of the situation and unpredictability of its outcomes, the use of scenario analysis by Hong Kong institutions and businesses in the lead up would appear to be a fairly obvious route to follow. However, teaching in the 'new' Hong Kong soon after the handback, where the economy was stagnant and uncertainty was in the air, and asking how many of the students' organizations had considered different scenarios for the post-handback world, not a single hand was raised. Rather, there was a sense of being lost and not in control.

In a similar vein, one of the most impactful events of the last decade, while not programmed into history like the Hong Kong change, was apparently not considered at all as a possibility by key stakeholders. The GFC has been much discussed and its impacts remain with us nearly a decade later. Looking back at the reactions of governments, financial institutions and the public as the crisis unfolded, it seems like there was no prior warning of events and that the financial collapse was as unpredictable as it was impactful. It may have been unpredictable in terms of its timing, and responses to it appear to have been ad hoc and ill-considered (cf. Alfaro and Kim, 2009/2010). However, there were plenty of signals in the environment and numerous voices expressing their concerns over the potential for – or even likelihood of – failure of the financial system (cf. Roeder, 2010). While these voices were ignored, a system in which power and reward were vested in stakeholders with a strong interest in maximizing short-term gains without concern for medium- to long-term consequences enabled – or, drove – a move towards an unsustainable and doomed global financial web of interconnections and interdependencies. Again, there appears to have been no consideration of alternative scenarios other than the one that stated that the system has worked very well for us this year, so it will work even better next year!

As we complete this text, the United Kingdom, Europe and the world wait anxiously to see how the UK vote to leave the European Union – the Brexit – will be implemented and with what consequences, socially and economically. Looking now at the aftermath of the referendum vote, it appears that none of the key powerful stakeholders in the UK – whether advocating to remain or to leave – had considered that the UK populace might actually vote to leave. Also, it appears from the (failed) calls for a second vote from the public, that many who wanted the country to remain part of the EU, did not vote at all, and some even voted to leave, on the assumption that a 'remain' result was a foregone conclusion.

Leaders from different sides of UK political structures have resigned since the vote, prompting the thought that none of them had a plan – a scenario – for dealing with a 'leave' vote. In the meantime, the political void appears to have left space for the emergence of social dysfunction. There has been a shocking rise in the reporting of race-hatred incidents, open expressions of minority xenophobic rhetoric and uncertainty for millions – both EU citizens in the UK and Britons living in Europe – as to the medium- and long-term implications. Summarizing the decision vacuum that exists immediately after the event, Tim Harford (2016) – writing in the influential *Financial Times* (FT) – called for the application of scenario planning, to move thinking, 'from "What will happen?" to "What will we do if it does?"'. As you read this text, there will be greater clarity about how and when Brexit will take place. But, has there been consideration of what the impacted and affected stakeholders will actually do?

There are numerous other examples that we can draw attention to, where there are or have been critical indicators of major events, yet there is no clear evidence that relevant stakeholders did previously consider or are now considering the key question of what they will do if and when it happens. These include the tragedy of 11 September 2001, where there were multiple indicators of possible major terror attack, yet there was no apparent coordinated response to try to identify it in detail and to prevent it. In late 2016, the United States stood on the verge of a controversial and divisive vote for President. Both candidates were popular with elements of their own parties and with sections of US society, but unloved by many others. They presented conflicting policy outlines on how the US would engage with its own people, its close neighbours and the world at large. However, there was little discussion on the future implications of Donald Trump gaining victory. As we know, President Trump quickly initiated controversial policy changes, including withdrawal from the TTP (see Chapter 3) and changing the US's relationship with Mexico. Rules on terms of office for President will allow Donald Trump to seek re-election in 2020, but not in 2024.

Conclusion

Our intent in this chapter has been to provide you with a set of accessible frameworks for inquiry into IB activities. These enable you to identify and compare the status of the full range of stakeholders that hold an interest in and/or power to impact any issue of interest to you. The models then help you to surface and examine the political, economic, etc. drivers that will determine how the future might unfold, as influenced by those with power and interest to bring about change. To consider these possible futures in a structured way, and to take account of the logics of causal and chronological relations between events, we outlined the application of scenario analysis, in particular CSM.

Based on your own use of these various models, whether for in-depth research of a critical issue or to provide a general overview of its potential implications, our aim is to inspire you to make your own judgements on the moral, ethical, societal and environmental impacts of organizational decisions, and hopefully to guide your own future actions towards 'the good of man' [*sic*] (Aristotle, 350BC/2004).

Questions

1. As you read this chapter, what is the current status of the UK's relationship with the EU? To what extent can you identify key powerful stakeholders' discussions of what might happen over the coming years, what they should do about it, and to whose benefit and whose disadvantage?
2. Based on the outcomes of the November 2016 US Presidential election, what is the current status of the US's relationship with Mexico? How has this impacted the business model of MNCs located in Mexico with factories adjacent to the US border? How has it impacted the lives and livelihoods of workers in these factories?
3. Select an IB activity that is of specific interest to you. What do you see as the critical uncertainties facing it over the next decade? How might these be resolved in different ways and how would these impact key stakeholders?

Further reading

As-Saber, S. and Cairns, G. (2015) '"Black international business" – critical issues and ethical dilemmas', in A. Pullen and C. Rhodes (eds), *The Routledge Companion to Ethics, Politics and Organizations*. Abingdon, UK: Routledge. pp. 119–131. Preview available at: https://books.google.com.au/books?hl=en&lr=&id=9SrLCQAAQBAJ&oi=fnd&pg=PA119&ots=yKtaXV1Hqq&sig=QDeOajWBMTg1lbj7dEuEDjqcjwo#v=onepage&q&f=false (accessed 22 September 2016).

Cairns, G., Śliwa, M. and Wright, G. (2010) 'Problematizing international business futures through a "critical scenario method"', *Futures*, 42: 971–97. Available at: http://dro.dur.ac.uk/6774/1/6774.pdf (accessed 22 September 2016).

Flyvbjerg, B. (undated) *What is Phronetic Planning Research? What is Phronetic Social Science?* Available at: http://flyvbjerg.plan.aau.dk/whatisphronetic.php (accessed 17 September 2016).

Concluding Remarks

In this short book, we have provided an overview of international business. In considering how we all affect or are affected by IB activities, we reflected upon the situation of a range of stakeholders, including employees, suppliers, broader society and the natural environment. We addressed examples of some of the less 'glamorous' and less widely debated forms of international business, such as race marketing and trade in arms, along with illicit and illegal practices such as tax evasion and people trafficking. As we come to the end of the project, we acknowledge some limitations. In outlining the field of IB across the contexts of time, space, theory and practice, we have obviously had to make choices about what to include and what to exclude. We therefore do not claim to offer a comprehensive account of IB, either with regard to the theories pertaining to the discipline or in relation to representations of IB practice. We have, however, directed you to further material that can trigger alternative interpretations of IB activity. We also provided some prompt questions to encourage you to think more widely about international business and its implications.

We hope that we have convinced you that it is important that we all reflect on how our thinking and acting as participants in IB affects others, the nature of the world and the possible outcomes for future generations. We trust that we have shown that the way things are now is not the only way they can be, and that there are options for a range of different futures. Primarily, we hope that we have made you think about how you can make a difference.

What have we done?

In offering an overview of the field of IB, we considered it necessary to provide an historical grounding. This shows how what is taken for granted and often presented as normal day-to-day IB activity is based upon centuries of development and perpetuation of practices that have their origins in European colonialism. In addition to enabling the accumulation of wealth by the colonizers, this process led to the suppression of indigenous populations in other territories and the appropriation and exploitation of the natural resources of their lands. We demonstrated that it is impossible to separate the present from the past. IB cannot be viewed as ahistorical and non-contextual – as a value-free activity of a purely economic nature, and as devoid of social and environmental impacts at a global level. Having outlined how European nation states were the early key actors that set the 'rules of the game', we argued that they established the basic principles that laid the ground for the emergence and dominance of the global MNC as the major contemporary power-broker of IB. In this context, we call now for a widening of participation in the debate in relation to the possibilities for alternative structures and forms of IB in the future.

Within the confines of this brief text, we offered a range of perspectives that take account of the different stakeholders involved in and affected by IB. In discussing examples of extant IB practices, we drew attention to the ephemeral nature of employment and income, the poor working conditions for many across the world, and the growth of socio-economic fragmentation and stratification at a global level. While we do not suggest that there is one 'right' way of conducting IB in answer to current problems, we aim to stimulate your thinking on the issues that we raise. We hope to provoke critical reflection on your own position within IB both now and in the future. In Chapters 6 and 7 we provided examples of frameworks that you can apply in undertaking a critical analysis of specific IB activities and issues.

How have we approached international business?

In engaging critically with the nature of contemporary IB, it is essential to consider it as a network of power relations. Contemplating the role of power, we see that, in many cases, IB activity is not based on equal exchange, but on very clear relationships of superior and subordinate. Our thinking on the nature and role of power leads us to contemplate the outcomes of IB activity: who does it benefit and who does it disadvantage? Who decides what is 'good' about IB, and according to whose definition of good is this determined?

Providing a philosophical foundation for our thinking on the good and bad of IB, we challenge the dominant neoliberal paradigm by reference to the Aristotelian concept of *phronēsis*, and the question of what is good for humanity in general? Contemporary interpretation of *phronēsis* in Flyvbjerg's (2001) four value-rational questions provides a framework for critical inquiry that is accessible, but also powerful in its ability for disclosure. These questions are:

1. Where are we going?
2. Is this desirable?

3. What, if anything, should we do about it?
4. Who gains and who loses, and by which mechanisms of power?

Reflecting on Flyvbjerg's questions, we address the impact of supranational institutions that set the context for IB, such as the IMF, the World Bank and the WTO. We question whether they act in the interests of broad civic society or are driven by those of a narrow section of the market. We also highlight the complex and dynamic relationships between other organizations and stakeholder groups that shape IB context and activity, such as NGOs, consumers and workers. Further, we recognize that answers to these questions need to be constantly revisited, as new politico-economic and technological disruptions give rise to previously unprecedented forms of IB activity and surface concomitant issues for debate.

As we have offered personal commentaries on the power dynamics of mainstream approaches to IB, we cannot deny our own influence on your thinking. We cannot ignore the power that we, as authors, exercise in relation to your interpretation of the issues that we write about. Please be aware of this as you form your own view of IB as a theoretical discipline and a domain of practice. In closing, we posit a final question, one that seeks to evoke a personal answer in you, our reader, informed by your own values, beliefs, hopes and aspirations.

Future directions

In this book, we discussed the historical growth of IB, with the caveat that history is not value-free and that narrating it is a matter of selection and interpretation. We also outlined some ideas about our present, as we write. However, your 'present' and future directions are for you to uncover. We ask that you appreciate how the future is not predictable, but the general direction of its development is knowable and understandable. While you must undertake your own research and analysis, let us offer a few thoughts to inspire your thinking. On the political front, a US Presidential election has been resolved and you know the basic tenure of the country in relation to its neighbours, its allies and its adversaries – ideological and economic. The politics of the EU and Brexit may be in a state of ongoing flux, with related social and economic effects and trends. Other areas of the world may have settled their conflicts, escalated them or be fostering new ones. The global economy has moved on, influenced by and impacting individual nations and the blocs we have discussed – EU, MERCOSUR, ASEAN and

NAFTA. How have the poorest nations fared under these changes? What is the state of power relations between MNCs and national governments under whatever new bilateral and multilateral trade agreements have been reached?

One technological trend that is to the fore as we complete our text is the development of autonomous vehicles – automobiles, boats, drones, etc. In different forms, these are seen as being of value for individual, commercial and military use. So, let us pose a few questions. First, how are new technologies performing, in terms of availability, cost and reliability? Second, to what ends are they being directed – for the benefit of broad humanity or in selective areas? Third, where they have been developed for commercial purposes, what has been their social and economic impact? In relation to these questions, we ask you to consider the following. If technological developments are now widely dispersed, are the economic benefits similarly shared? Where are the high-value aspects of design and intellectual property held? Where technology has replaced human labour, what has been the impact on employment and the lives of affected communities?

Finally, we are certain that climate change will remain a critical issue. Has there been action to seek to limit it and to militate against its worst impacts? The Arctic may be heading towards being ice-free all year. If so, has this brought change to sea freight logistics between the east of China and Europe? If ships travel across the Arctic to save time and fuel, how has this impacted major hub ports along traditional routes? At the same time, how have the low-lying coastal areas where most of the world's population live been impacted by changes to sea levels and to storm frequency and intensity – particularly in those poorer nations where both populations and agriculture are affected? You must be prepared to consider questions like this and to develop your own framework of inquiry for whatever complex and ambiguous issues you face.

Why does this matter to you?

International business is not a value-free activity that is devoid of social, economic and environmental impacts. Neither is it an activity that is conducted by 'others' and to which we are external bystanders. We all affect the nature and impact of IB and are affected by it on a daily basis, as consumers, employees and as citizens of the world. Therefore, we all have a responsibility to think about our own complicity in issues such as labour exploitation, tax avoidance and evasion, pollution and environmental degradation.

We argue that students of IB, and those who are and who aspire to be managers, must look beyond the superficial representations of IB as a field of practice, to consider the values and beliefs of those who perpetuate it and who are the major beneficiaries of it. In exploring the underlying and often unstated assumptions about the purpose of IB, we should refer to Flyvbjerg's final question: 'Who gains and who loses, and by which mechanisms of power?' As individuals, we must reflect critically upon what we do, how and why we do it, and what impact our actions have, or may have in the future, both locally and globally.

So, why *does* this matter to you?

References

Aeroxchange.com (2015) *About Aeroxchange*. Available at: www.corp. aeroxchange.com/index.php/about-us/about-aeroxchange (accessed 14 April 2016).

Alfaro, L. and Kim, R. (2009/2010) *U.S. Subprime Mortgage Crisis: Policy Reactions (B)*. Boston, MA: Harvard Business School Publishing.

Alldridge, P. (2015) 'Tax avoidance, tax evasion, money laundering and the problem of "offshore"', in S. Rose-Ackerman and P. Lagunes (eds), *Greed, Corruption and the Modern State: Essays in Political Economy*. Cheltenham, UK: Edward Elgar. pp. 317–335.

Alon, I., Jaffe, E., Prange, C. and Vianelli, D. (2016) *Global Marketing: Contemporary Theory, Practice, and Cases*. London: Routledge.

Americans for Tax Fairness (2014) *Walmart on Tax Day. How Taxpayers Subsidize America's Biggest Employer and Richest Family*. April. Available at: www.americansfortaxfairness.org/files/Walmart-on-Tax-Day-Americans-for-Tax-Fairness-1.pdf (accessed 10 September 2016).

Amnesty International (2016) *Child Labour Behind Smart Phone and Electric Car Batteries*, 19 January. Available at: www.amnesty.org/en/latest/news/2016/01/Child-labour-behind-smart-phone-and-electric-car-batteries/ (accessed 10 September 2016).

Aristotle (350BC/2004) *The Nicomachean Ethics*, trans. J.A.K. Thomson, 1953; Rev. H. Tredennick 1976. London: Penguin Books.

As-Saber, S. and Cairns, G. (2015) '"Black international business" – critical issues and ethical dilemmas', in A. Pullen and C. Rhodes (eds), *The Routledge Companion to Ethics, Politics and Organizations*. Abingdon, UK: Routledge. pp. 119–131.

Aston, H. (2016) 'Booming housing market increasingly a target for drug money launderers, say police', *The Sydney Morning Herald*, 22 January. Available at: www.smh.com.au/federal-politics/political-news/booming-housing-market-increasingly-a-target-for-drug-money-laun ders-say-police-20160122-gmc6ad.html (accessed 12 April 2016).

Ayres, C.J. (2012) 'The international trade in conflict minerals: Coltan', *Critical Perspectives on International Business*, 8(2): 178–193.

Baack, D.W., Harris, E.G. and Baack, D.E. (2012) *International Marketing*. Thousand Oaks, CA: Sage.

BAE Systems (2016) *What We Stand For*. Available at: www.baesystems. com/en/our-company/corporate-responsibility/working-responsibly/what-we-stand-for (accessed 10 September 2016).

Balassa, P. (1962) *The Theory of Economic Integration*. London: Allen and Unwin.

Banerjee, S.B. (2014) 'A critical perspective on corporate social responsibility: Towards a global governance framework', *Critical Perspectives on International Business*, 10(1–2): 84–95.

Banerji, R. (2016) 'In the dark: What is behind India's obsession with skin whitening?', *New Statesman*, 28 January. Available at: www.new statesman.com/politics/feminism/2016/01/dark-what-behind-india-s-obsession-skin-whitening (accessed 10 September 2016).

bangladeshaccord.org (2015) *Official Signatories, Accord on Fire and Building Safety in Bangladesh*. Available at: www.bangladeshaccord. org/signatories/ (accessed 12 April 2016).

Baran, P.A. (1957) *The Political Economy of Growth*. New York: Monthly Review Press.

Bartley, T. (2007) 'Institutional emergence in an era of globalization: The rise of transnational private regulation of labor and environmental conditions', *American Journal of Sociology*, 113(2): 297–351.

Bauman, Z. (1998) *Globalization: The Human Consequences*. Cambridge: Polity Press.

BBC (2014) 'Iraq Blackwater: US jury convicts four of 2007 killings', *BBC News*, 22 October. Available at: www.bbc.com/news/world-us-canada-29727314 (accessed 10 September 2016).

BBC (2016) 'Panama Papers: Denmark to buy leaked data', *BBC News*, 7 September. Available at: www.bbc.co.uk/news/world-latin-america-37299637 (accessed 9 September 2016).

Becker, J. (2014) 'Child laborers. In America. In 2014', *Politico*, 17 September. Available at: www.hrw.org/news/2014/09/17/child-laborers-america-2014 (accessed 26 May 2016).

Bondy, K., Matten, D. and Moon, J. (2008) 'MNC codes of conduct: Governance tools for CSR?', *Corporate Governance: An International Review*, 16(4): 294–311.

Brautigam, D. (2015) *Will Africa Feed China?* Oxford: Oxford University Press.

Bretton Woods Project (2005) *What are the Bretton Woods Institutions?* Available at: www.brettonwoodsproject.org/item.shtml?x=320747 (accessed 27 January 2008).

Brownell, K.D. and Warner, K.E. (2009) 'The perils of ignoring history: Big tobacco played dirty and millions died. How similar is big food?', *The Milbank Quarterly*, 87(1): 259–294.

BSCI (2016) *What We Do*. Available at: www.bsci-intl.org/content/what-we-do-0 (accessed 17 September 2016).

Bukharin, N. (1917/1987) *Imperialism and the World Economy*. London: Merlin.

Büthe, T. (2010) 'Private regulation in the global economy: A (p)review', *Business and Politics*, 12(3): 1–23.

Butler, S. (2013) 'One in six Walmart factories in Bangladesh fail safety review', *The Guardian*, 18 November. Available at: www.theguardian.com/business/2013/nov/18/walmart-bangladesh-factories-fail-safety-review (accessed 10 September 2016).

Cairns, G. and Śliwa, M. (2008) 'The implications of Aristotle's *phronēsis* for organizational inquiry', in D. Barry and H. Hansen (eds), *The Sage Handbook of New Approaches to Organization Studies*. Thousand Oaks, CA: Sage. pp. 318–331.

Cairns, G., Śliwa, M. and Wright, G. (2010) 'Problematizing international business futures through a "critical scenario method"', *Futures*, 42: 971–979.

Cardoso, F.H. (1972) 'Dependency and development in Latin America', *New Left Review*, 74: 83–95.

Cave, T. and Rowell, A. (2014) 'The truth about lobbying: 10 ways big business controls government', *The Guardian*, 12 March. Available at: www.theguardian.com/politics/2014/mar/12/lobbying-10-ways-corporations-influence-government (accessed 10 September 2016).

Cerdin, J.-L. and Selmer, J. (2014) 'Who is a self-initiated expatriate? Towards conceptual clarity of a common notion', *The International Journal of Human Resource Management*, 25(9): 1281–1301.

Chakrabortty, A. (2013) 'The woman who nearly died making your iPad', *The Guardian*, 5 August. Available at: www.theguardian.com/commentisfree/2013/aug/05/woman-nearly-died-making-ipad (accessed 10 September 2016).

Chakravartty, P. and Downing, J.H. (2010) 'Media, technology and the global financial crisis', *International Journal of Communication*, 4: 693–695.

Clemente, J. (2015) 'Choose Shell over Greenpeace for Arctic oil and natural gas', *Forbes*, 2 August. Available at: www.forbes.com/sites/judeclemente/2015/08/02/choose-shell-over-greenpeace-for-arctic-oil-and-natural-gas/#309f35b8136a (accessed 12 April 2016).

Constantine, M. (2016) 'Lush founder: Voters said they don't want our EU staff – we'll grow our business in Germany instead', *Bournemouth Echo*, 7 July. Available at: www.bournemouthecho.co.uk/news/14601945.Lush_founder__Voters_said_they_don_t_want_our_EU_staff___we_ll_grow_our_business_in_Germany_instead/ (accessed 17 September 2016).

Corporate Watch (2016) *Arms Trade*. Available at: www.corporatewatch.org/articles/arms-trade (accessed 10 September 2016).

Cotula, L., Vermeulen, S., Leonard, R. and Keeley, J. (2009) *Land Grab or Development Opportunity: Agricultural investment and International Land Deals in Africa*. London: IIED/FAO/IFAD.

Davidson, D. (2015) 'Illegal downloading throttles Australia', *The Australian*, 22 July. Available at: www.theaustralian.com.au/business/media/illegal-downloading-throttles-australia/news-story/b148f25 835bcaef0e25c8a892d112a2c (accessed 24 May 2016).

DeFillippi, R. and Arthur, M.B. (1994) 'Boundaryless contexts and careers: A competency-based perspective', in M.B. Arthur and D.M. Rousseau (eds), *The Boundaryless Career*. New York: Oxford University Press. pp. 116–131.

Donaghey, J. and Teague, P. (2006) 'The free movement of workers and social Europe: Maintaining the European ideal', *Industrial Relations Journal*, 37: 652–666.

Donaghey, J., Reinecke, J., Niforou, C. and Lawson, B. (2014) 'From employment relations to consumption relations: Balancing labor governance in global supply chains', *Human Resource Management*, 53(2): 229–252.

Dowling, G. (2014) 'The curious case of corporate tax avoidance: Is it socially irresponsible?', *Journal of Business Ethics*, 124: 173–184.

Duff, E. (2015) 'AFP reveals sex trafficking based in Sydney brothels', *The Sydney Morning Herald*, 13 September. Available at: www.smh.com.au/nsw/afp-reveals-sex-trafficking-based-in-sydney-brothels-2015 0912-gjkzwt.html (accessed 12 April 2016).

Dunne, J. (1993) *Back to the Rough Ground: Practical Judgment and the Lure of Technique*. Notre Dame, IN: University of Notre Dame Press.

Dunning, J. (1977) 'Trade, location of economic activity and the NINE: A search for an eclectic approach', in B. Ohlin, P.O. Hesselborn and P.M. Wijkman (eds), *The International Allocation of Economic Activity*. London: Macmillan. pp. 395–431.

Dunning, J. (1980) 'Toward an eclectic theory of international production: Some empirical tests', *Journal of International Business Studies*, 11(1): 9–31.

Dunning, J. (1981) *International Production and the Multinational Enterprise*. London: Allen & Unwin.

Dunning, J. (2000) 'The eclectic paradigm as an envelope for economic and business theories of MNE activity', *International Business Review*, 9: 163–190.

Durham, R.B. (2015) *Supplying the Enemy: The Modern Arms Industry & the Military-Industrial Complex*. New Delhi: RBD Publications.

Economist, The (2009) *The World in 2010: BRICS and BICIS*, 26 November. Available at: www.economist.com/blogs/theworldin2010/2009/11/acronyms_4 (accessed 13 September 2016).

Economist, The (2015) *Where Islamic State Gets its Money*. Available at: www.economist.com/blogs/economist-explains/2015/01/economist-explains (accessed 14 April 2016).

Egan, T. (2014) 'The corporate daddy. Walmart, Starbucks and the fight against inequality', *The New York Times*, 19 June. Available at: www.nytimes.com/2014/06/20/opinion/timothy-egan-walmart-starbucks-and-the-fight-against-inequality.html?_r=0 (accessed 10 September 2016).

Egels-Zandé́n, N. and WahlQvist, E. (2007) 'Post-partnership strategies for defining corporate responsibility: The business for social compliance initiative', *Journal of Business Ethics*, 70(2): 175–189.

Elkington, J. (1998) *Cannibals with Forks: The Triple Bottom Line of 21st Century Business*. Stony Creek, CT: New Society Publishers.

Elliott, L. (2014) 'Mint condition: Countries tipped as the next economic powerhouses', *The Guardian*, 9 January. Available at: www.theguardian.com/business/2014/jan/09/mint-condition-countries-tipped-economic-powerhouses (accessed 12 April 2016).

Faulconbridge, G. and Saul, J. (2015) 'Islamic State oil is going to Assad, some to Turkey, U.S. official says', *Reuters*, 10 December. Available at: www.reuters.com/article/us-mideast-crisis-syria-usa-oil-idUSKBN0TT2O120151210 (accessed 14 April 2016).

Flyvbjerg, B. (2001) *Making Social Science Matter: Why Social Inquiry Fails and How it Can Succeed Again*. Cambridge: Cambridge University Press.

Fortune (2016) *Fortune Global 500*. Available at: www.beta.fortune.com/global500/ (accessed 10 September 2016).

Frank, A.G. (1978) *Dependent Accumulation and Underdevelopment*. London: Macmillan.

Fransen, L. and Burgoon, B. (2012) 'A market for worker rights: Explaining business support for international private labour regulation', *Review of International Political Economy*, 19(2): 236–266.

Freeman, R.E. (1984) *Strategic Management: A Stakeholder Approach*. Boston: Pitman.

Freeman, R.E. (1994) 'The politics of stakeholder theory: Some future directions', *Business Ethics Quarterly*, 4(4): 409–421.

Freeman, R.E. and Reed, D.L. (1983) 'Stockholders and stakeholders: A new perspective on corporate governance', *California Management Review*, 25(3): 88–106.

Freeman, R.E., Harrison, J.S. and Wicks, A.C. (2007) *Managing for Stakeholders: Survival, Reputation, and Success*. New Haven, CT: Yale University Press.

Friedman, M. (1962) *Capitalism and Freedom*. Chicago, IL: University of Chicago Press.

Friedman, M. and Friedman, R. (1980) *Free to Choose: A Personal Statement*. London: Secker & Warburg.

Gates Foundation (2016) *Who We Are*. Available at: www.gatesfoundation.org/Who-We-Are/General-Information/Foundation-Factsheet (accessed 17 September 2016).

Gellman, B. (2012) 'Anonymous: Hackers', *Time*, 18 April. Available at: www.content.time.com/time/specials/packages/article/0,28804, 2111975_2111976_2112122,00.html (accessed 14 April 2016).

Gençsü, I. and Hino, M. (2015) 'Raising ambition to reduce international aviation and maritime emissions', *The New Climate Economy*, London and Washington. Available at: www.2015.newclimatee conomy.report/wp-content/uploads/2015/09/NCE-Aviation-Maritime_final.pdf (accessed 10 September 2016).

Glaser, A. (2015) 'You did it! Shell abandons Arctic drilling', *Greenpeace News*. Available at: www.greenpeace.org/international/en/news/Blogs/makingwaves/save-the-arctic-shell-abandons-arctic-drilling/blog/54263/ (accessed 12 April 2016).

Goldenberg, S. (2015) 'Work of prominent climate change denier was funded by energy industry', *The Guardian*, 21 February. Available at: www.theguardian.com/environment/2015/feb/21/climate-change-denier-willie-soon-funded-energy-industry (accessed 10 September 2016).

Goldstein, R. (2012) 'Time for a reality check on skin lightening creams', *The Conversation*, 11 September. Available at: www.theconversation.com/time-for-a-reality-check-on-skin-lightening-creams-7770 (accessed 10 September 2016).

Greenpeace (2015) *About Greenpeace*. Available at: www.greenpeace.org/international/en/about/ (accessed 12 April 2016).

Guardian, The (1999) 'Keeping Indonesia at arm's length', *The Guardian*, 8 September. Available at: www.theguardian.com/news/1999/sep/08/1 (accessed 12 April 2016).

Harding, L. (2016) 'What are the Panama Papers? A guide to history's biggest data leak', *The Guardian*, 5 April. Available at: www.theguardian.com/news/2016/apr/03/what-you-need-to-know-about-the-panama-papers (accessed 10 September 2016).

Harford, T. (2016) 'Brexit and the power of wishful thinking', *FT Magazine*, 13 July. Available at: www.ft.com/content/e8793d78-4880-11e6-8d68-72e9211e86ab (accessed 27 August 2016).

Healy, P. and Palupu, K. (2008/2016) 'The fall of Enron', *Harvard Business School*. Available at: www.hbs.edu/faculty/Pages/item.aspx?num=36626 (accessed 9 September 2016).

Heckscher, E. (1919/1950) 'The effect of foreign trade on the distribution of income', in H. Ellis and L.A. Metzler (eds), *Readings in the Theory of International Trade*. London: Allen and Unwin. pp. 272–300.

Hill, J. (2015) 'TPP's clauses that let Australia be sued are weapons of legal destruction, says lawyer', *The Guardian*, 10 November. Available at: www.theguardian.com/business/2015/nov/10/tpps-clauses-that-let-australia-be-sued-are-weapons-of-legal-destruction-says-lawyer (accessed 10 September 2016).

Hines, A. (2012) 'Walmart sex discrimination claims filed by 2,000 women', *Huffington Post*, 7 June. Available at: www.huffingtonpost.com.au/entry/walmart-sex-discrimination-women-_n_1575859.html?section=australia (accessed 10 September 2016).

Hobson, J.A. (1902/1938) *Imperialism: A Study*. London: George Allen and Unwin.

Hodal, K. (2013) 'Thailand racism row reignited by Unilever ad for skin-whitening cream', *The Guardian*, 27 October. Available at: www.theguardian.com/world/2013/oct/27/thailand-racism-unilever-skin-whitening-cream-citra (accessed 10 September 2016).

Hollensen, S. (2016) *Global Marketing*. Harlow: Pearson Education.

Hufbauer, G.C. (1970) 'The impact of national characteristics and technology on the commodity composition of trade in manufactured goods', in R. Vernon (ed.), *The Technology Factor in International Trade*. New York: Columbia University Press. pp. 145–231.

Human Rights Watch (2015) *At Your Own Risk. Reprisals Against Critics of World Bank Group Projects*. Available at: www.hrw.org/report/2015/06/22/your-own-risk/reprisals-against-critics-world-bank-group-projects (accessed 10 September 2016).

Hymer, S. (1960/1976) *The International Operations of National Firms: A Study of Direct Foreign Investment*. Cambridge, MA: MIT Press.

ILSR (2013) *Walmart's Assault on the Climate. The Truth behind One of the Biggest Climate Polluters and Slickest Greenwashers in America*, November. Available at: www.ilsr.org/wp-content/uploads/2013/10/ILSR-_Report_WalmartClimateChange.pdf (accessed 10 September 2016).

IMF (2016) *About the IMF*. Available at: www.imf.org/external/about.htm (accessed 10 September 2016).

Inman, P. (2013) 'WTO agreement condemned as deal for corporations, not world's poor', *The Guardian*, 7 December. Available at: www.theguardian.com/world/2013/dec/07/wto-global-trade-deal-condemned-poverty (accessed 10 September 2016).

Ito, T. (2012) 'Can Asia overcome IMF stigma?', *The American Economic Review*, 102(3): 198–202.

Jevons, W.S. (1871) *The Theory of Political Economy*. London: Macmillan.

Johanson, J. and Vahlne, J.-E. (1977) 'The internationalization process of the firm – a model of knowledge development and increasing foreign market commitments', *Journal of International Business Studies*, 8(1): 23–32.

Johanson, J. and Vahlne, J.-E. (2009) 'The Uppsala internationalization process model revisited: From liability of foreignness to liability of outsidership', *Journal of International Business Studies*, 40(9): 1411–1431.

Johnson, T. (2015) 'Palm oil companies exploit Indonesia's people – and its corrupt political machine', *The Guardian*, 11 June. Available at: www.theguardian.com/sustainable-business/2015/jun/11/palm-oil-industry-indonesia-corruption-communities-forests (accessed 10 September 2016).

Kahane, A. (2007) 'Between an ostrich and a flamingo', *Mail & Guardian*, 12 April. Available at: www.mg.co.za/article/2007-04-12-between-an-ostrich-and-a-flamingo (accessed 10 September 2016).

Kar-Gupta, S. and Guernigou, Y.L. (2007) 'BNP freezes $2.2bln of funds over subprime', *Reuters Funds News*, 9 August. Available at: www.uk.reuters.com/article/bnpparibas-subprime-funds-idUKGRI92603020070809 (accessed 10 September 2016).

Kessler, I. and Bach, S. (2011) 'The citizen-consumer as industrial relations actor: New ways of working and the end-user in social care', *British Journal of Industrial Relations*, 49: 80–102.

Klein, N. (2002) *Fences and Windows: Dispatches from the Front Lines of the Globalization Debate*. New York: Picador USA.

Knowles, K. (2015) '10 of the biggest complaints about Uber – from Uber drivers', *The Memo*, 5 November. Available at: www.thememo.com/2015/11/05/uber-driver-complaints-uberpeople-net-black-cab/ (accessed 12 April 2016).

Knudsen, J.S. (2013) 'The growth of private regulation of labor standards in global supply chains: Mission impossible for western small- and medium-sized firms?', *Journal of Business Ethics*, 117(2): 387–398.

Krugman, P. (1979) 'A model of innovation, technology transfer, and the world distribution of income', *The Journal of Political Economy*, 87(2): 253–266.

Krugman, P. (1981) 'Intraindustry specialization and the gains from trade', *Journal of Political Economy*, 89: 959–973.

Krugman, P. (2012) *End This Depression Now!* New York: W.W. Norton & Company.

Krugman, P. (2015) 'The case for cuts was a lie: Why does Britain still believe it? The austerity delusion', *The Guardian*, 29 April. Available at: www.theguardian.com/business/ng-interactive/2015/apr/29/the-austerity-delusion (accessed 10 September 2016).

Leigh, D. and Evans, R. (2010) 'BAE admits guilt over corrupt arms deals', *The Guardian*, 6 February. Available at: www.theguardian.com/world/2010/feb/05/bae-systems-arms-deal-corruption (accessed 10 September 2016).

Lenin, V.I. (1902/1969) *What Is To Be Done? – Burning Questions of our Movement*. New York: International Publishers.

Li, D. (2015) 'Migrant workers and the US military in the Middle East', *Middle East Report*, Summer. Available at: www.merip.org/mer/mer275/migrant-workers-us-military-middle-east (accessed 10 september 2016).

Linder, S.B. (1961) *An Essay on Trade and Transformation*. New York: John Wiley.

Loacker, B. and Śliwa, M. (2016) '"Moving to stay in the same place?" Academics and theatrical artists as exemplars of the "mobile middle"', *Organization* 23(5): 657–679.

Lodge, G. and Wilson, C. (2006) *A Corporate Solution to Global Poverty: How Multinationals Can Help the Poor and Invigorate Their Own Legitimacy*. Princeton, NJ: Princeton University Press.

McSmith, A. (2009) 'The firm with a "back door key to Number 10"', *The Independent*, 2 October. Available at: www.independent.co.uk/news/business/news/the-firm-with-a-back-door-key-to-number-10-1796377.html (accessed 11 September 2016).

Malalo, H. and Jorgic, D. (2016) 'Uber driver attacked in Kenya, his taxi torched: Police', *Reuters Technology News*, 22 February. Available at: www.reuters.com/article/us-kenya-security-idUSKCN0VV19X (accessed 14 April 2016).

Markusen, J.R. (1998) 'Multinational firms, location and trade', *The World Economy*, 21: 733–756.

Marlow, B. (2016) 'World economy stands on the cusp of another crash, warns Lord Mervyn King', *The Telegraph*, 27 February. Available at: www.telegraph.co.uk/business/2016/02/26/world-economy-stands-on-the-cusp-of-another-crash-warns-lord-mer/ (accessed 14 April 2016).

Marshall, A. and Marshall, M.P. (1879/1994) *The Economics of Industry*. Bristol: Thoemmes.

Marx, K. and Engels, F. (1848/2002) *The Communist Manifesto*. London: Penguin.

Menger, C. (1871/1950) *Principles of Economics*. Glencoe, IL: The Free Press.

Miller, J.W. and Mauldin, W. (2016) 'U.S. imposes 266% duty on some Chinese steel imports', *Wall Street Journal*. Available at: www.wsj.com/articles/u-s-imposes-266-duty-on-some-chinese-steel-imports-1456878180 (accessed 10 September 2016).

Milmo, C. (2015) 'Government invites regimes with "appalling" human rights records to London arms fair', *The Independent*, 10 September. Available at: www.independent.co.uk/news/uk/politics/government-invites-regimes-with-appalling-human-rights-records-to-london-arms-fair-10495415.html (accessed 10 September 2016).

Monbiot, G. (1996) *Hawks and Doves*. Available at: www.monbiot.com/1996/07/30/hawks-and-doves/ (accessed 10 September 2016).

Moore, E. (2012) 'Civets, brics and the next 11', *Financial Times*, 8 June. Available at: www.ft.com/cms/s/0/c14730ae-aff3-11e1-ad0b-00144feabdc0.html#axzz4Js43jqfn (accessed 10 September 2016).

Mundy, K. and Menashy, F. (2014) 'The World Bank and private provision of schooling: A look through the lens of sociological theories of organizational hypocrisy', *Comparative Education Review* 58(3): 401–27.

Murphy, E. (1999) 'Character and virtue ethics in international marketing: An agenda for managers, researchers, and educators', *Journal of Business Ethics*, 18(1): 107–124.

Neate, R. (2016) 'Strong Walmart earnings add $5bn to Walton family fortune', *The Guardian*, 18 February. Available at: www.theguardian.com/business/2016/feb/18/walmart-revenues-walton-fortune-minimum-wage (accessed 10 September 2016).

OECD (2008) 'Declaration of the Summit on Financial Markets and the World Economy', *OECD/G20*, 15 November. Available at: www.oecd.org/g20/summits/washington-dc/declarationofthesummitonfinancial marketsandtheworldeconomy.htm (accessed 9 September 2016).

Ohlin, B. (1933/1967) *Interregional and International Trade*. Cambridge, MA: Harvard University Press.

Olsson, M. (2012) 'Chinese "land grabs" in Africa – the reality behind the news', *SIANI Policy Brief*. Available at: www.siani.se/sites/clients.codepositive.com/files/document/siani_policy_brief_-_chinese_land_grabs_in_africa_130204_web.pdf (accessed 9 September 2016).

O'Neill, J. (2001) 'Building better global economic BRICS', *Global Economics Paper No 66*. Available at: www.goldmansachs.com/our-thinking/archive/archive-pdfs/build-better-brics.pdf (accessed 9 September 2016).

O'Neill, J. and Stupnytska, A. (2005) 'The long-term outlook for the BRICs and N-11 post crisis', *Global Economics Paper No 192*. Available at: www.goldmansachs.com/our-thinking/archive/brics-at-8/brics-the-long-term-outlook.pdf (accessed 10 September 2016).

Open Secrets (2016a) *Influence and Lobbying. Top Organization Contributors*. Available at: www.opensecrets.org/orgs/list.php?cycle=ALL (accessed 10 September 2016).

Open Secrets (2016b) *Influence and Lobbying. BAE Systems*. Available at: www.opensecrets.org/lobby/clientsum.php?id=D000000583&year=2015 (accessed 12 September 2016).

Open Secrets (2016c) *Lobbyists Representing Bechtel Group: 2016*. Available at: www.opensecrets.org/lobby/clientlbs.php?id=D000000237 (accessed 14 September 2016).

Oxfam (2014) *A Dangerous Diversion: Will the IFC's Flagship Health PPP Bankrupt Lesotho's Ministry of Health?* Available at: www.oxfam.org/sites/www.oxfam.org/files/file_attachments/bn-dangerous-diversion-lesotho-health-ppp-070414-en_0.pdf (accessed 10 September 2016).

Oxfam (2016) *An Economy for the 1%: How Privilege and Power in the Economy Drive Extreme Inequality and How This Can be Stopped*.

Available at: www.policy-practice.oxfam.org.uk/publications/an-economy-for-the-1-how-privilege-and-power-in-the-economy-drive-extreme-inequ-592643 (accessed 10 September 2016).

Oxfam International (2016) *History of Oxfam International*. Available at: www.oxfam.org/en/countries/history-oxfam-international (accessed 14 April 2016).

Pan, K.Y. (2013) *MINT: the new BRIC on the block?* Available at: http://blogs.ft.com/beyond-brics/2013/11/14/mint-the-new-bric-on-the-block/ (accessed 6 April 2017).

Porter, M. (1985) *Competitive Advantage: Creating and Sustaining Superior Performance*. New York: Free Press.

Porter, M. (1990) *The Competitive Advantage of Nations*. New York: Free Press.

Prahalad, C.K. (2005) *The Fortune at the Bottom of the Pyramid: Eradicating Poverty Through Profits*. Upper Saddle River, NJ: Wharton School Publishing.

Prebisch, R. (1971) *Change and Development – Latin America's Great Task: Report Submitted to the Inter-American Development Bank*. New York: Praeger.

Rangan, V.K., Quelch, J.A., Herrero, G. and Barton, B. (2007) (eds) *Business Solutions for the Global Poor*. San Francisco, CA: Jossey-Bass.

Rawlinson, K. and Peachey, P. (2012) 'Hackers step up war on security services: GCHQ has been threatened with cyber-attack tomorrow', *The Independent*, 13 April. Available at: www.independent.co.uk/news/uk/crime/hackers-step-up-war-on-security-services-7640780.html (accessed 14 April 2016).

Reich, R. (2015) *Why the Trans-Pacific Partnership Agreement is a Pending Disaster*. Available at: www.robertreich.org/post/107257859130 (accessed 10 September 2016).

Reuters (2010) 'After BRICs, look to CIVETS for growth - HSBC CEO', *Reuters – Market News*, 27 April. Available at: www.uk.reuters.com/article/hsbc-emergingmarkets-idUSLDE63Q26Q20100427 (accessed 13 September 2016).

Ricardo, D. (1817) *On the Principles of Political Economy and Taxation*. London: John Murray.

Riisgaard, L. and Hammer, N. (2011) 'Prospects for labour in global value chains: Labour standards in the cutflower and banana industries', *British Journal of Industrial Relations*, 49(1): 168–190.

RNZ (2012) 'Greenpeace guilty of misleading advertising', *Radio New Zealand News*, 4 April. Available at: www.radionz.co.nz/news/national/102510/greenpeace-guilty-of-misleading-advertising (accessed 12 April 2016).

Roeder, M. (2010) *The Big Mo: Why Momentum now Rules our World*. Sydney: ABC Books/Harper Collins.

RT.com (2014) 'Blackwater founder: We could have fought ISIS if Obama hadn't "crushed my old business"', 22 September. Available at: www.rt.com/usa/189684-blackwater-private-army-isis/ (accessed 10 September 2016).

Santos, N. and Laczniak, G.R. (2009) 'Marketing to the poor: An integrative justice model for engaging impoverished market segments', *Journal of Public Policy and Marketing*, 28(1): 3–15.

Save the Children (2016a) *What We Do*. Available at: www.healthynewborn network.org/partner/save-the-children/ (accessed 17 September 2016).

Save the Children (2016b) *Newborn Health. Improving Newborn Survival*. Available at: www.savethechildren.org/site/c.8rKLIXMGI pI4E/b.6234293/k.7FC1/Newborn_Health.htm (accessed 17 September 2016).

Say, J.B. (1803/2001) *A Treatise on Political Economy*. Edison, NJ: Transaction Publishers.

Schmelzer, M. (2010) 'Marketing morals, moralizing markets: Assessing the effectiveness of fair trade as a form of boycott', *Management & Organizational History*, 5(2): 221–250.

Schoofs, M. (2002) 'Physicians' group defies patent law to bring AIDS drugs to South Africa', *The Wall Street Journal*, 30 January. Available at: www.wsj.com/articles/SB1012338297451348120 (accessed 29 August 2016).

Sea Shepherd (2015) 'Sea Shepherd found guilty by Danish courts of defending pilot whales', *Sea Shepherd News & Media*, 7 August. Available at: www.seashepherd.org/news-and-media/2015/08/07/sea-shepherd-found-guilty-by-danish-court-of-defending-pilot-whales-1728 (accessed 12 April 2016).

Segall, L. (2014) 'Peter Thiel: Uber is "most ethically challenged company in Silicon Valley"', *CNN Money*, 18 November. Available at: www. money.cnn.com/2014/11/18/technology/uber-unethical-peter-thiel/ (accessed 12 April 2016).

Sen, A.K. (1983) 'Development: Which way now?', *Economic Journal*, 93(372): 745–762.

Sen, A.K. (1999) *Development as Freedom*. New York: Knopf.

Shabi, R. (2015) 'Looted in Syria – and sold in London: The British antiques shops dealing in artefacts smuggled by ISIS', *The Guardian*, 3 July. Available at: www.theguardian.com/world/2015/jul/03/antiquities-looted-by-isis-end-up-in-london-shops (accessed 14 April 2016).

Sharp, G. (2011) 'Q&A: Gene Sharp', *Aljazeera – Politics*, 6 December. Available at: www.aljazeera.com/indepth/opinion/2011/12/201112 113179492201.html (accessed 13 September 2016).

Shotter, J. and Tsoukas, H. (2014) 'Performing phronesis: On the way to engaged judgment', *Management Learning*, 45(4): 377–396.

Sikka, P. and Willmott, H. (2010) 'The dark side of transfer pricing: Its role in tax avoidance and wealth retentiveness', *Critical Perspectives on Accounting*, 21: 342–356.

SIPRI (2016a) *Arms Trade. Top List TIV* Tables. Available at: www.arm strade.sipri.org/armstrade/page/toplist.php (accessed 10 September 2016).

SIPRI (2016b) *World Military Spending Resumes Upward Course, Says SIPRI*. Available at: www.sipri.org/media/press-release/2016/ world-military-spending-resumes-upward-course-says-sipri (accessed 14 September 2016).

Sirait, M.K. (2009) *Indigenous People and Oil Palm Plantation Expansion in West Kalimantan, Indonesia*. Den Haag: Cordaid Memisa.

Slattery, G. (2016) 'Chile's head of Transparency International resigns after "Panama Papers"', *Reuters*, 4 April. Available at: www.reuters. com/article/panama-tax-chile-idUSL2N1771Z1 (accessed 9 September 2016).

Smith, A. (1776/1999) *An Inquiry into the Nature and Causes of the Wealth of Nations*. London: Penguin.

Smith, D. (2009) 'The food rush: Rising demand in China and west sparks African land grab', *The Guardian*, 3 July. Available at: www. theguardian.com/environment/2009/jul/03/africa-land-grab (accessed 9 September 2016).

Sourcewatch (2006a) 'History', *Vinnell Corporation*. Available at: www.sourcewatch.org/index.php/Vinnell_Corporation (accessed 11 September 2016).

Sourcewatch (2006b) 'In Saudi Arabia', *Vinnell Corporation*. Available at: www.sourcewatch.org/index.php/Vinnell_Corporation (accessed 11 September 2016).

Spiegel Online International (2013) 'How legalizing prostitution has failed', *Der Spiegel*, 30 May. Available at: www.spiegel.de/international/ germany/human-trafficking-persists-despite-legality-of-prostitution-in-germany-a-902533.html (accessed 12 April 2016).

Steger, M. (2013) *Globalization: A Very Short Introduction*. Oxford: Oxford University Press.

Sum, N.-L. and Jessop, B. (2015) *Towards a Cultural Political Economy: Putting Culture in its Place in Political Economy*. Cheltenham, UK: Edward Elgar.

Telegraph, The (2011) 'Top 10 most commonly used word, phrases and names', *The Telegraph*, 10 November. Available at: www.telegraph.co.uk/ news/newstopics/howaboutthat/8881312/Top-10-lists-most-commonly-used-word-phrases-and-names.html (accessed 14 April 2016).

Tett, G. (2010) 'The story of the BRICS', *FT Magazine*, 15 January. Available at: www.ft.com/content/112ca932-00ab-11df-ae8d-00144 feabdc0 (accessed 12 April 2016).

Torrens, R. (1815) *Essay on the External Corn Trade*. London: J. Hatchard.

Transparency International (2013) *Business Principles for Countering Bribery*. Berlin: Transparency International.

Transparency International (2015a) *What is Corruption?* Available at: www.transparency.org/what-is-corruption/ (accessed 12 April 2016).

Transparency International (2015b) *Lobbying in Europe. Hidden Influence, Privileged Access*. Available at: www.transparency.org/what wedo/publication/lobbying_in_europe (accessed 10 September 2016).

Traxler, F. (1999) 'The state in industrial relations: A cross-national analysis of developments and socioeconomic effects', *European Journal of Political Research*, 36(1): 55–85.

Uber.com (2016a) 'Get there – Your day belongs to you', *Uber Become a Driver*. Available at: www.uber.com/ (accessed 14 April 2016).

Uber.com (2016b) 'Open roles', *Uber Careers*. Available at: www.uber. com/careers/list/?city=&country=&keywords=&subteam=&team (accessed 14 April 2016).

United Nations (2015) 'GDP and its breakdown at current prices in US dollars', United Nations Statistics Division, December. Available at: http://unstats.un.org/unsd/snaama/dnllist.asp (accessed 10 September 2016).

UNODC (undated) *Factsheet on Human Trafficking*. Available at: www. unodc.org/documents/human-trafficking/UNVTF_fs_HT_EN.pdf (accessed 12 April 2016).

UNODC (2011) *Estimating Illicit Financial Flows Resulting from Drug Trafficking and Other Transnational Organized Crimes*, Research Report. Available at: www.unodc.org/documents/data-and-analysis/ Studies/Illicit_financial_flows_2011_web.pdf (accessed 12 April 2016).

Vernon, R. (1966) 'International investment and international trade in the product life cycle', *Quarterly Journal of Economics*, 80 (2): 190–207.

Vidal, P. (2015) 'The emigration of health-care workers: Malawi's recurring challenges', *Migration Information Source*, 21 October. Available at: www.migrationpolicy.org/article/emigration-health-care-workers-malawis-recurring-challenges (accessed 14 September 2016).

Vinnell Arabia (2016) *About Vinnell Arabia*. Available at: www.vinnel larabia.com/Main/aboutus (accessed 11 September 2016).

Wallerstein, I. (1974) *The Modern World-System*. New York: Academic Press.

Wallerstein, I. (2004) *World-Systems Analysis: An Introduction*. Durham, NC: Duke University Press.

Walmart (2015a) *Walmart 2015 Annual Report. Winning the Future of Retail – One Customer at a Time.* Available at: http://s2.q4cdn.com/056532643/files/doc_financials/2015/annual/2015-annual-report.pdf (accessed 10 September 2016).

Walmart (2015b) *Global Responsibility Report.* Available at: http://corporate.walmart.com/global-responsibility/global-responsibility-report (accessed 10 September 2016).

Walras, L. (1874) *Eléments D'économie Politique Pure, ou théorie de la richesse sociale (Elements of Pure Economics, or the theory of social wealth).* Lausanne: F. Rouge.

War on Want (2016) *Our Work.* Available at: www.waronwant.org/our-work (accessed 12 April 2016).

Watkins, K. (2015) 'What next for poor countries fighting to trade in an unfair world?', *The Guardian.* Available at: www.theguardian.com/global-development/2015/dec/22/doha-round-world-trade-organisation-nairobi-poor-countries (accessed 10 September 2016).

Williams, L. (2015) 'What is TTIP? And six reasons why the answer should scare you', *The Independent,* 6 October. Available at: www.independent.co.uk/voices/comment/what-is-ttip-and-six-reasons-why-the-answer-should-scare-you-9779688.html (accessed 10 September 2016).

Wilson, D. and Purushothaman, R. (2003) 'Dreaming with BRICs: The path to 2050', *Global Economics Paper No 99.* Available at: www.goldmansachs.com/our-thinking/archive/archive-pdfs/brics-dream.pdf (accessed 9 September 2016).

World Bank (1989) *About Us: Articles of Agreement.* Available at: http://web.worldbank.org/WBSITE/EXTERNAL/EXTABOUTUS/ 0,,content MDK:20049563~pagePK:43912~menuPK:58863~piPK:36602,00.html#11 (accessed 7 November 2007).

World Bank (1990) *World Development Report 1990: Poverty.* Washington, DC: The World Bank/Oxford University Press.

World Bank (2015) *World Bank Forecasts Global Poverty to Fall Below 10% for First Time; Major Hurdles Remain in Goal to End Poverty by 2030,* 4 October. Available at: www.worldbank.org/en/news/press-release/2015/10/04/world-bank-forecasts-global-poverty-to-fall-below-10-for-first-time-major-hurdles-remain-in-goal-to-end-poverty-by-2030 (accessed 10 September 2016).

World Bank (2016) *What We Do.* Available at: www.worldbank.org/en/about/what-we-do (accessed 10 September 2016).

Wright, G. and Cairns, G. (2011) *Scenario Thinking: Practical Approaches to the Future.* Basingstoke, UK: Palgrave Macmillan.

WTO (2015) *Trade and Tariffs. Trade Grows as Tariffs Decline.* Available at: www.wto.org/english/thewto_e/20y_e/wto_20_brochure_e.pdf (accessed 10 September 2016).

Index